# BAPTISM
# THROUGH THE
# CENTURIES

Henry F. Brown

Pacific Press Publishing Association, Mountain View, California
Omaha, Nebraska

# Preface

The author's special interest in the history of the rite of baptism began some years ago when he visited some of the ancient baptisteries of Europe, with their great variety of shapes and sizes. These baptisteries seemed to suggest that they had a story to tell about the development of the doctrine of baptism itself. He wondered if anyone had made a definitive study of baptism from the archaeological viewpoint.

Later he discovered such a study—*The Archaeology of Baptism,* by Wolfred Nelson Cote, published in 1876. This book provided much valuable information, which aided greatly in the preparation of this newer volume.

The author of *Baptism Through the Centuries* has included a large amount of quoted material, for he wishes to allow Church Fathers, Reformers, historians, and other witnesses to speak for themselves. The reader may draw his own conclusions on the basis of the testimony presented.

Mr. Brown's investigation will undoubtedly aid the reader in his knowledge of the historical background of various forms of baptism. In addition, it is hoped that the reader will be enabled more intelligently to appraise his own relationship to this doctrine which has been of importance to Christians through the centuries.

THE PUBLISHERS.

# Contents

# Ancient Purification Rites

### ❦ 1 ❦

Many primitive tribes and races practice some kind of initiatory rites. Admission into the tribe, consecration to the priesthood, or attainment of adulthood, may be the occasion for such ceremonies. Often there is some form of blood offering; either the blood of the candidate himself or that of an animal is sacrificed.

Other initiation rites involve purification, which is usually accomplished with water or fire. The ancient pagans practiced a form of water baptism as one of their purification rites.

"That a ritual washing away of sin characterized other religions than the Christian, the Fathers of the church were aware, and Tertullian notices, in his tract *On Baptism* (ch. v.), that the votaries of Isis and Mithras were initiated *per lavacrum,* 'through a font,' and that in the *Ludi Apollinares et Eleusinii, i.e.* the mysteries of Apollo and Eleusis, men were baptized (*tinguntur,* Tertullian's favorite word for baptism), and, what is more, baptized, as they presumed to think, 'unto regeneration and exemption from the guilt of their perjuries.' 'Among the ancients,' he adds, 'anyone who stained himself with homicide went in search of waters that could purge him of his guilt.' "[1]

Tertullian writes that the heathen used baptism in the mysteries of their gods, "and they presume that the effect of their doing that is their regeneration, and the remission of the penalties due to their perjuries." He concluded that the devil was imitating the things of God; "we find him, too, practising baptism in his [subjects]."[2]

Mithraism, a mystic Oriental religion, also practiced a form of ablution. "They believed themselves purified of their guilt by the ritual ablutions, and this baptism lightened their conscience of the weight of their heavy responsibility."[3]

Among the Jews purification by water washings was well known. The Levitical system of worship was of "divers washings." Hebrews 9:10. The priests were washed as they began their sacred service. Exodus 29:4. Each priest must wash before he entered upon his daily service. Exodus 30:19, 20. The people were ordered to "wash their clothes." Exodus 19:10. An "unclean" person who approached the camp was to "wash himself with water." Deuteronomy 23:11. David cried out in his repentance, "Wash me throughly from mine iniquity." "Wash me, and I shall be whiter than snow." Psalm 51:2, 7. Isaiah pleaded, "Wash you, make you clean; put away the evil of your doings." Isaiah 1:16. Naaman was ordered to wash himself seven times in the Jordan. 2 Kings 5:10. Jeremiah calls to Jerusalem, "O Jerusalem, wash thine heart from wickedness, that thou mayest be saved." Jeremiah 4:14.

The rabbis instructed their followers in the practice of baptism: "The Rabbis connect with this [the washing of the clothes] the duty of bathing by complete immersion."[4]

Immersion was also demanded of proselytes. "One of the steps in becoming a proselyte was complete immersion in running water to wash away impurities acquired while in a state of heathenism. . . . It is probable that in course of time the ritual bath was considered less and less as the means of purification from physical uncleanliness, and more and more as a cleansing from spiritual impurity—from sin."[5]

The Babylonian Talmud (*Mass Jevamoth,* fol. 47) relates that "when a proselyte is received, he must be circumcised; and then when he is cured (of the wound of circumcision) they baptize him in the presence of two wise men, saying, Behold he is an

Israelite in all things."[6] Again (*Tract. Repudii*), "Israel does not enter into covenant but by these three things, by circumcision, baptism, and peace offering; and proselytes, in like manner."[7]

To the Jews the figure of the new birth was familiar, though Jesus gave it a new and deeper significance. When a pagan became a Jew he was considered as born into the family of Abraham; but this was largely in a legal sense, while Jesus taught that the new birth was a spiritual regeneration. "If any one become a proselyte, he is like a child new born."[8] He was "washed" in the water. "Whenever, in the law, washing of the flesh, or of the clothes, is mentioned, it means nothing else than dipping the whole body in a laver; for if a man dips himself all over except the tip of his little finger, he is still in his uncleanness."[9].

"The oldest of the Christian sacraments appear to owe much to Judaism. Baptism seems clearly not to have been a Christian innovation. It had been used as a Jewish initiatory rite for proselytes."[10]

Thus, when John the Baptist appeared, "he came into all the country about Jordan, preaching the baptism of repentance for the remission of sins." Luke 3:3. Notice his encounter with Jewish authorities: "This is the record of John, when the Jews sent priests and Levites from Jerusalem to ask him, Who art thou? . . . that we may give an answer to them that sent us. What sayest thou of thyself?" John 1:19-22. He was not questioned on the ceremony he was performing. The point under discussion was simply, By what authority do you demand of us another baptism?

Thus challenged, John's answer was, "He . . . sent me to baptize with water." John 1:33. He did not pretend that God had just originated the rite, or prescribed for John the details of its administration. But John was sent to baptize those who responded to his message, and he made use of a ceremony already known to his converts.

John baptized at Aenon near Salim, "because there was much

water there." John 3:23. He baptized by immersion in harmony with the accepted method of purification.

"Jesus Himself was baptized by John and He esteemed John's baptism highly. It appears also as if many of John's disciples had gone over into Jesus' following. Hence John's baptism was taken up into primitive Christianity in its original significance of a washing away of the uncleanness of the old aeon, a cleansing necessary for the entry into the new Messianic world."[11]

Jesus submitted to John's baptism. "Suffer it to be so now," He said, in answer to John's hesitation: "for thus it becometh us to fulfill all righteousness." Matthew 3:15. The Galilean made no explanation as to the meaning of baptism, or its form or implications. He accepted the baptism then practiced, and His disciples baptized in the same way. John 3:22; 4:1, 2. He commanded His disciples to baptize their converts wherever they taught His gospel. Matthew 28:19, 20.

The apostle Paul explained the rite of baptism in more detail: "We are buried with Him by baptism into death," he wrote, "that like as Christ was raised up from the dead by the glory of the Father, even so we also should walk in newness of life. For if we have been planted together in the likeness of His death, we shall be also in the likeness of His resurrection." Romans 6:4, 5.

Paul was himself baptized in Damascus by the disciple Ananias. Then, obedient to the commission of Christ, he spread the practice wherever he taught, preached, and converted men to Christ. According to Paul's teachings baptism means much more than merely a symbol of purification, which it had been since time immemorial. It means more than merely an initiatory rite to enter the fellowship of believers, though it was this also. It was an announcement voluntarily made by the convert, many times in the midst of persecutions, that he was burying his past life, with its heathen vices or its Jewish pride and complacency, to enter into a new realm of spiritual life. "Therefore if any man be in Christ, he is a new creature: old things are passed away; behold, all things are become new." 2 Corinthians 5:17.

Baptism thus became a sign of a revolutionary transformation in the individual, not merely a transfer of loyalties from pagan gods to Christ or from Mosaic rituals to Christian doctrines. It was a ceremony that cut across social life, and many times domestic life, as cleanly as would a surgeon's scalpel. Adolph Harnack states that the ceremony of the individual's immersion and emergence from the water served as a guarantee that old things were now washed away and gone, leaving him a new man.[12]

# Baptism in the Second and Third Centuries

### ✺ 2 ✺

By the end of the first century, the last of Christ's apostles had died. But Christianity was firmly established, and it continued to grow despite persecution. The pagan religions, with their beautiful temples and colorful liturgy, still profoundly influenced life in the far-flung Roman Empire. Emperor worship was sporadically enforced as a sign of loyalty. Christianity was a proscribed sect, hated and informed on by the Jews and, under certain of the emperors, feared and hunted down by the pagans. The intellectual leaders in those times were the philosophers of different schools.

Mithraism was a vigorous missionary religion from Persia which had been introduced a century earlier. In many teachings and customs it strangely paralleled Christianity, much to the embarrassment of the Christians. "The Fathers themselves were first to recognize that 'the devil too had his sacraments,' and that the Eleusinian, Isiac, Mithraic and other *mystae* used baptism in their rites of initiation."[1]

Christians at this time had no schools. They had little organization above the local level and no books except for a few tracts which were later called "gospels" and some copies of old letters of Peter and Paul that circulated, hand copied, from place to place. Christianity was largely a personal experience spontaneously shared by individuals.

"The chief agents in the expansion of Christianity appear not to have been those who made it a profession or a major part of their occupation, but men and women who earned their livelihood in some purely secular manner and spoke of their faith to those whom they met in this natural fashion. Thus when Celsus denounces a religion which spreads through workers in wool and leather and fullers and uneducated persons who get hold of children privately and of ignorant women and teach them, Origen does not deny that this occurs."[2]

Inasmuch as the early Christians had no school of theology, it is not to be wondered at that changes gradually occurred. Rather, it is surprising that more profound distortions did not occur during the first 200 years. The apostle Paul had foretold an apostasy and insisted that it had already begun in his day. Speaking to the elders, he said:

"Take heed therefore unto yourselves, and to all the flock, over the which the Holy Ghost hath made you overseers, to feed the church of God, which He hath purchased with his own blood. For I know this, that after my departing shall grievous wolves enter in among you, not sparing the flock. Also of your own selves shall men arise, speaking perverse things, to draw away disciples after them." Acts 20:28-30.

"Let no one deceive you by any means. For it will not come until after the Great Apostasy, and the revealing of the Man of Sin, the son of perdition, the adversary, who opposes and exalts himself against all that is called God, or is an object of worship; so that he takes his seat in the Temple of God, and vaunts himself as God. Do you not recall that I often told you this, when I was with you? And now you know what is holding him back, to the end that he may be revealed in his appointed time. For the mystery of lawlessness is already at work; only there is one who is hindering and will continue till he be removed; and then the lawless one will be revealed." 2 Thessalonians 2:3-8, *The New Testament in Modern English, Centenary Translation*, Philadelphia: The Judson Press, 1924.

Whereas Paul stated that "the mystery of iniquity doth already work" about A.D. 52, a generation later John said clearly, "Now are there many antichrists." 1 John 2:18.

As many of the pagan converts accepted Christianity without thorough indoctrination, they retained many of their heathen ideas. Philosophers, too, accepted Christianity, and they naturally gravitated into positions of leadership in thought, though often they had changed the tenor of their thinking but little. Their writings give evidence of the retention of numerous heathen concepts.

Our information on the development of Christian thought and practice during the two centuries following the death of Paul is fragmentary, and we have no clear record of just how some of the later practices of the church began to develop during this time. "We know even less of the spread of Christianity in the second century than we do of its propagation in the first century," says Latourette.[3] The vigorous, Spirit-filled, enthusiastic movement almost disappears, and we later find that the adherents of Christianity are a different group of people. The writings of the Church Fathers, both authentic and spurious, make it painfully apparent that apostasy occurred, as foretold by Paul. The Fathers, leaders of the early Christian church, often erred, but one can learn from their writings what was believed and taught in the early church.

Many "gospels" and "epistles" made their appearance in the early days of the church. They usually carried the name of some apostle or other prominent leader. But the style of writing and the absurd stories of magic and miracles mark them for what they are—clumsy fiction.

The source of the growing pagan influences within Christianity is described as follows by Hatch:

"During the earliest centuries of Christianity, the mysteries, and the religious societies which were akin to the mysteries, existed on an enormous scale throughout the eastern part of the Empire. There were elements in some of them from which Christianity recoiled, and against which the Christian Apologists use the language of strong invective. But, on the other hand, the majority of them had the same aims as Christianity itself—the aim of worshipping a pure God, the aim of living a pure life, and the aim of cultivating the spirit of brotherhood. They were part of a great religious revival which distinguishes the age.

"It was inevitable when a new group of associations came to exist side by side with a large existing body of associations, from which it was continually detaching members, introducing them into its own midst with the practices of their own original societies impressed upon their minds, that this new group should tend to assimilate, with the assimilation of their members, some of the elements of these existing groups. This is what we find to have been in fact the case. . . . The influence of the mysteries, and of the religious cults which were analogous to the mysteries, was not simply general; they modified in some important respects the Christian sacraments of Baptism and the Eucharist. . . .

"These were the simple elements of early Christian baptism. When it emerges after a period of obscurity—like a river which flows under the sand—the enormous changes of later times have already begun."[4]

The Church Fathers, sensing the need of some substitute for the "mysteries" which were so much a part of the lives of the people, placed the rite of baptism in this category. "From the third century it [baptism] became one of the secret mysteries of the church."[5]

The *Clementine Homilies* mention baptism frequently. Chapter XIX, dealing with "Privileges of the baptised," says:

"In the present life, washing in a flowing river, or a fountain, or even in the sea, with the thrice-blessed invocation, you shall not only be able to drive away the spirits which lurk in you; but yourselves no longer sinning, and undoubtingly believing God, you shall drive out evil spirits and dire demons, with terrible diseases, from others."[6]

Another interesting document, which dates from about the first of the second century—the *Didache,* or the *Teaching of the Twelve Apostles*—says:

"Regarding baptism, baptize thus. . . . 'Baptize in the name of the Father, and of the Son, and of the Holy Spirit' in running water. But, if you have no running water, baptize in any other; and, if you cannot in cold water, then in warm. But, if the one is lacking, pour the other three times on the head 'in the name of the Father, and Son, and Holy Spirit.' "[7]

Roman Catholic editors of this work have added as a footnote: "Baptism was usually by immersion of the whole body."

Justin Martyr (*ca.* 115-165), a convert to Christianity, wrote an *Apology* for his new faith, in which he described baptism as it was practiced in his time:

"I will also relate the manner in which we dedicated ourselves to God when we had been made new through Christ; lest, if we omit this, we seem to be unfair in the explanation we are making. As many as are persuaded and believe that what we teach and say is true, and undertake to be able to live accordingly, are instructed to pray and to entreat God with fasting, for the remission of their sins that are past, we praying and fasting with them. Then they are brought by us where there is water, and are regenerated in the same manner in which we were ourselves regenerated. For, in the name of God, the Father and Lord of the universe, and of our Saviour Jesus Christ, and of the Holy Spirit, they then receive the washing with water. . . .

"There is pronounced over him who chooses to be born again, and has repented of his sins, the name of God the Father and Lord of the universe; he who leads to the laver the person that is to be washed calling by this name alone. . . . And this washing is called illumination, because they who learn these things are illuminated in their understandings. And in the name of Jesus Christ, who was crucified under Pontius Pilate, and in the name of the Holy Ghost, who through the prophets foretold all things about Jesus, he who is illuminated is washed."[8]

"Not a few ideas from analogous rites of pagan mysteries crept into the teaching of the theologians."[9] Tertullian frankly confesses, "We are thrice immersed, making a somewhat ampler pledge than the Lord has appointed in the Gospel."[10]

Basil, from the fourth century, is more explicit in his admission:

"For we are not, as is well known, content with what the Apostle or the Gospel has recorded; but, both before and after, we say other words as having great importance for the mystery, and these we derive from unwritten teaching."[11]

Tertullian says that an "enlargement" was made to the rite:

"Grant that, in days gone by, there was salvation by means of bare faith, before the passion and resurrection of the Lord. But now that faith has been enlarged, and is become a faith which believes in His nativity, passion, and resurrection, there has been an amplification added to the sacrament."[12]

Some of these "amplifications" introduced by the Fathers are as follows: The water itself was considered as having an important part in the sacrament. It must be running water, if possible. The water was blessed. Cyprian (*ca.* 200-258) held this concept of the magical effect of water on the candidate: "It is required, then," he wrote, "that the water should first be cleansed and sanctified by the priest, that it may wash away by its baptism the sins of the man who is baptized."[13] This blessing of the water was mentioned as early as *The Apostolical Constitutions.*[14]

The effect of this blessing of the water changed the waters magically, says Tertullian.[15] Cyril of Alexandria stated that "the water is transmuted or changed in its nature, by the Holy Ghost, to a sort of divine and ineffable power."[16] Cyprian called it "saving water."[17] The water, then, was magical and had an effect on the candidate. He was said to be "illuminated." The pagan Roman believed the water removed "some natural state of the person using it,"[18] and this was the idea widely accepted in Christianity. Subsequently Pope Leo the Great went further in defining it thus:

"Baptism makes a change not only in the water, but in the man that receives it; for thereby Christ receives him, and he receives Christ; and he is not the same, after baptism, that he was before; but the body of him that is regenerated is made the flesh of Him that was crucified."[19]

Early in the history of baptism the idea gained currency that, because of its supernatural nature, the rite could not be repeated. Athanasius (*ca.* 296-373) as a boy was playing with other boys on the seashore. Bishop Alexander witnessed their sport and noticed that they were imitating the baptismal ritual. The youth Athanasius had baptized several of his playmates. The old bishop, after questioning the boys, accepted the baptism as genuine and had the boys put into school to be trained by priests.[20]

Thus the heresy of salvation by water baptism was taught, rather than salvation in Christ through repentance. Tertullian (*ca.* 150-*ca.* 240) made bold to say, "The prescript is laid down that 'without baptism, salvation is attainable by none,'"[21] and Irenaeus (*ca.* 120-*ca.* 200) identified baptism with regeneration.[22]

Cyprian (*ca.* 200-258) stated the matter thus: "One is not born by the imposition of hands when he receives the Holy Ghost, but in baptism, that so, being already born, he may receive the Holy Spirit."[23] Thus baptism developed into a sacrament and became one of the "mysteries" of the Christian religion.

The next step was the teaching that once regenerated by baptism, one cannot lose that grace.

In time compulsory baptism was introduced. If there is no salvation without baptism, and if a man once baptized cannot lose this grace even if he wishes to, why not oblige men to be baptized even against their wishes? Thus the baptizer does the unwilling candidate an eternal favor. This practice, says Schaff, dated from Justinian's reign. [24] Charlemagne used this logic in offering to the Saxons the choice of massacre by troops, or baptism by the priests.[25]

Fasting was believed by some to be essential to baptism. As early as the times of the *Didache* it was ordered, "Before the baptism, let the one who baptizes and the one to be baptized fast. . . . You shall require the person being baptized to fast for one or two days."[26]

The *Encyclopaedia Britannica* describes the rite in the early centuries as follows:

"(b) They were subjected to a scrutiny and prepared, as today in the western churches the young are prepared for confirmation. . . .

"(c) They were again and again exorcized, in order to rid them of the lingering taint of the worship of demons.

"(d) Some days or even weeks beforehand they had the creed recited to them. . . .

"(e) There followed an act of unction, made in the East with the oil of the catechumens blessed only by the priest, in the West with the priest's saliva applied to the lips and ears. . . .

"(f) Renunciation of Satan. The catechumens turned to the west in pronouncing this; then turning to the east they recited the creed.

"(g) They stepped into the font, but were not usually immersed, and the priest recited the baptismal formula over them as he poured water, generally thrice, over their heads.

"(h) They were anointed all over with chrism or scented oil, the priest reciting an appropriate formula. Deacons anointed the males, deaconesses the females.

"(i) They put on white garments and often baptismal wreaths or chaplets as well. . . .

"(j) They received the sign of the cross on the brow; the bishop usually dipped his thumb in the chrism and said: 'In name of Father, Son and Holy Ghost, peace be with thee.' . . .

"(k) The first communion followed, with milk and honey added.

"(l) Usually the water in the font was exorcized, blessed and chrism poured into it, just before the catechumen entered it."[27]

Sponsors were assigned to the persons baptized. According to tradition, this custom was begun by Hyginus about A.D. 154.[28]

Hippolytus in Canon XIX gives some of the regulations for baptism in the early part of the third century:

"Unvesting of the candidates for baptism. . . .

"The candidate is directed to face westward and to renounce Satan.

"Unction by the presbyter with the oil of exorcism.

"The candidate faces eastward, and declares his belief in Father, Son, and Holy Spirit.

"Then he enters the water, and the presbyter, laying his hand on the candidate's head, immerses him thrice, asking him at each immersion whether he believes in the Three Persons of the Blessed Trinity. . . .

"Then the presbyter anoints him with the oil of thanksgiving, in the name of the Trinity, and in the form of the cross, on the forehead, mouth, breast, whole body, head, and face.

"The candidate is wiped, clothed, and introduced into the church.

"The bishop lays his hands on the heads of all the recently baptized, with prayer.

"The bishop signs each of them on the forehead with the sign of the cross, and gives to each the kiss of peace. . . .

"The candidates then partake of milk and honey. . . .

"They are now designated 'Christiani perfecti'—'perfect Christians.' "[29]

"The new converts were to be taught, that those are *born again* who are initiated by baptism into the Christian worship, and that they ought to exhibit in their conduct the innocence of little infants; and therefore *milk* and *honey,* the common food of infants, were administered to them."[30]

Robinson states that there were no fewer than twenty-two different parts in the baptismal ceremony: twelve in preparation, five at the administration itself, and five after the ceremony was completed.[31] Truly, as Tertullian confessed, they made "a somewhat ampler pledge than the Lord has appointed in the Gospel."

The validity of the baptism of heretics was a subject of controversy. Cyprian in Africa insisted on the rebaptism of those who had left their heresies to enter the orthodox church. Stephen, bishop of Rome, maintained the validity of any baptism.[32] Firmilian wrote (A.D. 256) to Cyprian and asked: "Do Stephen and they who agree with him approve of this also, especially when neither the symbol of the Trinity nor the legitimate and ecclesiastical interrogatory were wanting to her?"[33]

At a Synod of Carthage, probably held between 218 and 222, Cyprian of Carthage insisted on rebaptizing those who had been baptized by heretics. Pope Stephen opposed the practice, declaring he was following the primitive custom. Cyprian admitted that tradition was against him, but insisted that the tradition was "a human and unlawful tradition."[34]

An anonymous book appeared at this time, *De Rebaptismate*. It states that "the ordinances of Pope Stephen, forbidding the rebaptism of converts, are in accordance with antiquity and ecclesiastical tradition."[35]

In the second and third centuries, the time element entered the growing body of traditions relating to baptism. In New Testament times when a man was converted he was immediately baptized. The jailer was baptized at midnight; the eunuch was baptized by Philip in a pond by the side of the wilderness road when they came to a place with sufficient water. However, in the church influenced by the mysteries, baptismal services were deferred to certain feast days, such as Easter, Christmas, Epiphany, and Pentecost.

Another innovation was baptism by blood. Martyrs who, though not baptized, were sacrificed to satisfy the bloodlust of the populace, were considered as baptized in their own blood. Tertullian (*ca.* 160-*ca.* 240) says, "We *have* indeed, likewise, a *second* font, (itself withal *one* [with the former,]) of *blood*. . . . This is the baptism which both stands in lieu of the fontal bathing when that has not been received, and restores it when lost."[36] Fulgentius (A.D. 507) says none could be saved without baptism "except those who are for the name of Christ baptized in their own blood."[37] Cyprian (*ca.* 200-258) refuted this, saying: "Nor let anyone say, 'that he who accepts martyrdom is baptized in his own blood.' "[38]

"Clinical baptism" was the form of baptism given to a sick person who was sprinkled because he could not be immersed. However, baptism of the sick was for a time considered less than adequate. The Council of Neocaesarea (Canon XII) stated: "If any one be baptized when he is sick, . . . he cannot be promoted to the Presbyterate, unless on account of his subsequent zeal and faithfulness, or because of lack of men."[39]

Cyprian admitted clinical baptism with these words:

"You have asked also, dearest son, what I thought of those who obtain God's grace in sickness and weakness, whether they are to be accounted legitimate Christians, for that they are not washed, but sprinkled, with the saving water. . . . Nor ought it to trouble any one that sick people seem to be sprinkled or affused. . . . Whence it appears that the sprinkling also of water prevails equally with the washing of salvation."[40]

This statement is revelatory of two developments: First, sprinkling and pouring are considered equally efficacious. Second, baptism is not the submersion of the body, but simply the application of magic water to the candidate's head.

"There is evidence to show that those who received this rite in this form were somewhat despised; for the nicknames *clinici* and *grabatorii* were, unworthily Cyprian declares, bestowed on them by neighbors. . . . It was long of commending itself to ministers and people, and did not attain to almost general use until the 13th cent."[41]

"The Montanists baptized in the name of the Father and Son and Montanus and Priscilla."[42] The Arians in Jerome's time baptized in the name of the Creator and creatures.[43] The Anomaeans, a sect of Arians, baptized thus: "In the name of the uncreated God and in the name of the created Son, and in the name of the Sanctifying Spirit, procreated by the created Son."[44]

Thus baptism, the simple rite of entrance into the church of Christ, was by the time of the Council of Nicaea (A.D. 325) cluttered with numerous accretions from paganism. The baptism promulgated by Christ and the apostles was vastly different from the series of pagan liturgies that in time supplanted it.

# The Adoption
# of Trine Immersion

## ❧3❧

Of those Christians living today who have been immersed, a large number have been immersed three times. Of those who have been sprinkled, at least two-thirds have been sprinkled thrice. What is the origin of this practice?

In the extant writings from the first two centuries trine immersion is presented, without explanation, as an established practice. When did it originate? By whose authority was it done? The origins are hidden in the uncertain times following the death of Paul.

The *Didache,* which has been called "the oldest church manual," instructed the baptizer thus: "Pour the other [water] three times on the head 'in the name of the Father, and Son, and Holy Spirit.' "[1] Tertullian, at the beginning of the third century, argues: "He commands them to baptize into the Father and the Son and the Holy Ghost, not into a unipersonal God. And indeed it is not once only, but three times, that we are immersed into the Three Persons, at each several mention of Their names."[2] Again he says, "Hereupon we are thrice immersed, making a somewhat ampler pledge than the Lord has appointed in the Gospel."[3]

Justin (*ca.* 114-*ca* 165) in his *Apology* seems to imply trine immersion in saying, "There is pronounced over him . . . the name of God the Father. . . . And in the name of Jesus Christ,

(17)

. . . and in the name of the Holy Ghost."[4] This is believed to be the first mention of triple immersion.

Hippolytus, writing in the early part of the third century, says: "Then he enters the water, and the presbyter, laying his hand on the candidate's head, immerses him thrice, asking him at each immersion whether he believes in the Three Persons of the Blessed Trinity, successively, the presbyter repeating the formula of baptism at each immersion."[5]

Ambrose (died 397) addresses the converts thus: "Thou wast asked, . . . 'Dost thou believe in God the Father Almighty?' and thou repliedst, 'I believe;' and wast dipped, that is, buried. A second demand was made, 'Dost thou believe in Jesus Christ our Lord, and in his cross?' thou answeredst again, 'I believe;' and wast dipped. Therefore thou wast buried with Christ; for he that is buried with Christ, rises again with Christ. A third time the question was repeated, 'Dost thou believe in the Holy Ghost?' And thy answer was, 'I believe.' Then thou wast dipped a third time; that thy triple confession might absolve thee from the various offenses of thy former life."[6]

Bishop Munnulus, or Monulus, of Girba addressed the Council of Carthage in A.D. 256 in favor of trine immersion.[7] Augustine (died 430) also mentions trine immersion.[8] Jerome (died 420) said, "We are thrice dipped in water."[9]

*The Apostolical Constitutions* (date uncertain, possibly fourth century) enjoin, "If any bishop or presbyter does not perform the three immersions of the one admission, but one immersion, which is given into the death of Christ, let him be deprived [deposed]."[10]

Gelasius, the bishop of Caesarea (367-395), wrote: "Then let the priest baptize by trine immersion alone, invoking but once the Holy Trinity, and saying thus: 'And I baptize thee in the name of the Father,' and let him immerse once, 'and of the Son,' and let him immerse a second time, 'and of the Holy Ghost,' and let him immerse a third time."[11]

In Tertullian's time (*ca.* 160-*ca.* 240) in North Africa "the mode of baptism was by triple immersion in the font, which had been already blessed."[12]

"The early fathers," says a recognized authority, "without a voice to the contrary, believed that triple baptism was the New Testament form."[13] Another authority says, "The way of trine immersion, or plunging the head of the person three times into the water, was the general practice of all antiquity."[14]

A note in *A Select Library of Nicene and Post-Nicene Fathers* on Jerome's *Dialogue Against the Luciferians* says:

"Triple immersion, that is, thrice dipping the head while standing in the water, was the all but universal rule of the Church in early times. There is proof of its existence in Africa, Palestine, Egypt, at Antioch and Constantinople, in Cappadocia and Rome."[15]

How did this custom gain such acceptance? Says Bingham:

"The original of this custom is not exactly agreed upon by the ancients. Some derive it from apostolical tradition; others, from the first institution of baptism by our Saviour; whilst others esteem it only an indifferent circumstance or ceremony, that may be used or omitted, without any detriment to the sacrament itself, or breach of any Divine appointment."[16]

Martin of Braga (*ca.* 520-580) wrote *Epistola ad Bonifatium de trina mersione* in reply "to a letter from a Spanish bishop who supposed that the custom of triple aspersion in baptism was of Arian origin."[17]

Though the details of the origin of trine baptism may be obscure, there is much evidence that the source is paganism. As John Henry Newman frankly states, the Early Fathers "endeavored to connect their own doctrine with theirs, whether Jewish or pagan, adopting their sentiments and even their language, as far as they lawfully could."[18]

The pagans had analogous customs. "The threefold immersion in the threefold name, which had its counterpart in the heathen lustrations, was the rule among the Gentile Christians."[19]

Early writers do not attempt to find Scripture examples of trine immersion. Rather, the appeal is to tradition. Tertullian, after mentioning trine immersion and other ecclesiastical customs, confesses:

"If, for these and other such rules, you insist upon having positive Scripture injunction, you will find none. Tradition will be held forth to you as the originator of them, custom as their strengthener, and faith as their observer.[20]

"If no passage of Scripture has prescribed it," he says, "assuredly custom, which without doubt flowed from tradition, has confirmed it."[21]

Jerome is equally explicit in saying:

"For many other observances of the Churches, which are due to tradition, have acquired the authority of the written law, as for instance the practice of dipping the head three times in the laver, and then, after leaving the water, of tasting mingled milk and honey."[22]

Basil (*ca.* 330-*ca.* 379) professes no knowledge at all of the origin of trine immersion:

"Of the beliefs and public teachings preserved in the Church, some we have from written tradition, others we have received as delivered to us 'in a mystery' by the tradition of the Apostles; and both of these have in relation to true piety the same binding force. And these no one will gainsay, at least no one who is versed even moderately in the institutions of the Church. For were we to reject such customs as are unwritten as having no great force, we should unintentionally injure the gospels in their very vitals; or, rather, reduce our public definition to a mere name and nothing more. For example, to take the first and most general instance, who is there who has taught us to sign with the cross those who have trusted in the name of the Lord Jesus Christ? What writing has taught us to turn to the East in our prayers? Which of the saints has left us in writing the words at the invocation and at the displaying of the bread in the eucharist and the cup of blessing? For we are not, as is well known, content with what the Apostle or the Gospel has recorded; but, both before and after, we say other words as having great importance for the mystery, and these we derive from unwritten teaching. Moreover, we bless the water of baptism and the oil of chrism, and, besides this, him who is baptized. From what writings? Is it not from the silent and mystical tradition? What written word teaches the anointing of oil itself? And whence is it that a man is baptized three times? And as to other customs of baptism, from what Scripture comes the renunciation of Satan and his angels? Does not this come from the unpublished and secret teaching which our fathers guarded in silence, averse from curious meddling and inquisitive investigation, having learned the lesson that the reverence of the mysteries is best preserved in silence? How was it proper to parade in public the teaching of those things which it was not permitted the uninitiated to look at?"[23]

Eunomius (A.D. 360) taught a single immersion; he baptized only in the name of the death of Christ. This was considered an innovation and strongly condemned.[24] The historian Sozomen says he corrupted "in this manner, the apostolical tradition."[25]

After practicing trine immersion for centuries, the Western Church swung back to single immersion. The transformation cannot be traced in detail; only one council seems to have passed a canon on it. But it is known that Pope Gregory the Great (A.D. 590) permitted single immersion in Spain. At that time the Arians in Spain were practicing trine immersion to sustain their heresies, and Gregory advised the orthodox in this case to adopt single immersion.[26] This is noted in the Fourth Council of Toledo (A.D. 633):

"Because the sacrament of baptism is administered by some Spanish priests with three immersions, and by others with only one, . . . let us inform ourselves regarding the precepts of the Apostolic See. . . . Gregory, pontiff of the Roman church, . . . in consulting the most holy Bishop Leandro about this diversity that was followed in Spain, answered among other things: that regarding trine immersion, no better answer could be given than that they continue to do as they have been doing; because the different customs, having the same faith, does not endanger the holy church. We, therefore, employ trine immersion. . . . [This] does not contradict the practice of others who baptize with one immersion."[27]

No trace of trine immersion can be found in the Jewish religion, or in the practices of John the Baptist. However, there is considerable evidence of it in the paganism that dominated the world into which Christianity was born. Virgil speaks of it, Ovid mentions it twice, Persius and Horace tell of triple lustrations.[28]

"And on the last mentioned passage the scholiast Acro remarks: 'He uses the words *thrice purely,* because people in expiating their sins, plunge themselves in thrice.' Such examples of the ancient usage encounter us everywhere in Greek and Latin antiquity."[29]

Remembering that the leaders of the church, after the passing of the apostles, came from pagan backgrounds and that there were neither Christian books nor theological schools, one can more readily understand why they retained many of their pagan viewpoints and customs.

Trine immersion is but one of scores of these "ideas from the analogous rites of pagan mysteries [that] crept into the teachings of theologians."[30]

# The Introduction
# of Infant Baptism

## ❦ 4 ❦

John the Baptist preached a message of warning and judg-
ment, and demanded repentance. He insisted on seeing evidences
of reformation before baptizing a convert. Luke 3:8. The people
came "confessing their sins." Matthew 3:6. After immersion
John exhorted them, "saying unto the people, that they should
believe on Him which should come." Acts 19:4.

Later New Testament references reveal no essential change in
the manner of baptism, though the teachings of Jesus gave it a
deeper and broader meaning than John attached to it. "He that
believeth and is baptized shall be saved." Mark 16:16. The
three thousand on the Day of Pentecost were told to "repent, and
be baptized." Acts 2:38. Again, 5,000 "believed" before baptism.
Acts 4:4. More "believers were . . . added." Acts 5:14. A great
number of priests "were obedient to the faith." Acts 6:7. The
people "gave heed" to what Philip said. Acts 8:6. "They
believed" and "were baptized." Verse 12. Simon "believed" and
"was baptized." Verse 13. "If thou believest, . . . thou mayest,"
the Ethiopian was told, and he responded, "I believe." Acts 8:
37, 38.

"As it is easy to understand, in the first centuries of the Church
baptism was given to none but adults, after they had been well
instructed in the mysteries of the faith."[1]

"Among the many variations accompanying the history of

baptism, the most important was the transition from adult to infant baptism. . . . Evidence that a change was taking place is abundant in the third century. This change is one of the most significant that has passed over the history of the church. Adult baptism stood for the principle of individualism, demanding intelligence as the condition of repentance and faith, and the personal vow of obedience as the ground of its proper administration."[2]

Infants are mentioned many times in the New Testament. Baptism is also mentioned repeatedly, but the two are never spoken of together. Jesus took babes onto His lap and "laid His hands on them" (Matthew 19:15), but there is no hint of His having baptized them. One of the greatest apologists for infant baptism in all literature, William Wall, concedes in speaking of John (the same is true of Christ), "There is no express mention indeed of any children baptized by him."[3]

Those who advocate the baptism of infants usually quote admitted advocates, such as Origen and Cyprian, and then endeavor to trace the practice back through earlier writers. Often cited as an early endorsement of the practice is a statement by Justin Martyr about the year 150: "Many, both men and women, who have been Christ's disciples from childhood, remain pure at the age of sixty or seventy years."[4] Some maintain that being "Christ's disciples from childhood" refers to baptism in childhood.

Irenaeus wrote (*ca.* A.D. 185) that "[Jesus] came to save all through means of Himself—all, I say, who through Him are born again to God—infants, and children, and boys, and youths, and old men. He therefore passed through every age, becoming an infant for infants, thus sanctifying infants."[5]

Wall says of this statement, "This is the first express mention that we have met with of infants baptized."[6] It should be noted, however, that baptism is here only inferred, *not* specifically mentioned.

There is no ambiguity in Tertullian's reference to baptism of infants. Writing at the close of the second century, he is the earliest of the church fathers to write unequivocally on the subject—and he is opposed to the practice:

"Delay of baptism is preferable; principally, however, in the case of little children. . . . The Lord does indeed say, 'Forbid them not to come unto Me.' Let them 'come,' then, while they are growing up; let them 'come' while they are learning, while they are being taught whither to come; let them become Christians when they have become able to know Christ. Why does the innocent period of life hasten to the 'remission of sins?' More caution will be exercised in worldly matters: so that one who is *not* trusted with earthly substance *is* trusted with divine! Let them know how to 'ask' for salvation, that you may seem [at least] to have given 'to him that asketh.' "[7]

In Tertullian's view, even widows and unmarried young people were too unstable to baptize. "If any understand the weighty import of baptism," he wrote, "they will fear its reception more than its delay: sound faith is secure of salvation."[8]

Of this outspoken statement, Neander comments:

"In the latter years of the second century, Tertullian appeared as a zealous opponent of infant baptism, a proof that it was not then usually considered as an apostolical ordinance, for in that case he would hardly have ventured to speak so strongly against it."[9]

Among the strongest evidences that infant baptism was not the practice in the early church are the Fathers' statements urging deferment of baptism. It was common in those centuries to postpone baptism until near the hour of death, as it was thought that sins committed after baptism were unforgivable. Ambrose (*ca.* 340-397) was the son of Christian parents, yet at the age of thirty-four he was unbaptized. A bishop was needed, and the mob howled for "Ambrose for bishop!" He was elected, baptized, consecrated, and elevated to the bishopric, all in the same week! *The Catholic Encyclopedia* says: "Strange to say, like so many other believers of that age, from a misguided reverence for the sanctity of baptism, he was still only a catechumen, and by a wise provision of the canons ineligible to the episcopate."[10]

Another great Church Father, Augustine (354-430), was not baptized until the age of thirty-three. His mother Monica refused to have him baptized as a child although he clamored for it.[11]

Gregory of Nazianzus was an adult when he was baptized,[12] as was also his intimate friend Basil.[13] Nectarius, successor to Gregory of Nazianzus, was, like Ambrose, baptized after he was elected bishop of Constantinople.[14] Chrysostom was in his twenties when baptized.[15] Constantine postponed baptism until just before his death.[16] Jerome was baptized after he was twenty.[17]

As late as 340 Gregory Theologus suggests the age of three for baptism.[18] Augustine said that fourteen was the earliest that people were ordinarily baptized on their own profession.[19] During this period the *Constitutions of the Apostles* warned, "But he that says, When I am dying I will be baptized, lest I should sin and defile my baptism, is ignorant of God, and forgetful of his own nature."[20]

The first Church Father of whom we have record definitely to advocate infant baptism was Origen (*ca.* 185-*ca.* 254), who wrote that "infants also are by the usage of the church baptized."[21] "Infants are baptized for the forgiveness of sins."[22] "The church had from the apostles a tradition to give baptism even to infants."[23]

In the opinion of the historian Harnack, "It was easy to justify child baptism, as he recognized something sinful in the corporeal birth itself, and believed in sin which had been committed in a former life. The earliest justification of child baptism may therefore be traced back to a philosophical doctrine."[24]

Cyprian, bishop of Carthage for some ten years before his martyrdom in 258, was the next leading advocate of the immersion of babes. One of the country bishops, Fidus, wrote him regarding the baptism of infants. Should he wait until the eighth day as did the Jews in circumcision? Cyprian, surrounded by sixty-six bishops of North Africa, decided that the child should not necessarily wait, but be baptized if necessary as soon as it was born.[25]

The first council to prescribe infant baptism was the Sixteenth

Council of Carthage (418): "If any man says that new-born children need not be baptized, . . . let him be anathema."[26]

Thus historical evidences point to the fact that infant baptism originated in North Africa, and through the influence of Augustine (354-430) soon permeated Christendom. Wrote Augustine:

"The custom of our mother church in baptizing infants must not be disregarded, nor be accounted needless, nor believed to be other than a tradition of the apostles."[27]

He further says:

"Which the whole body of the church holds, as delivered to them, in the case of little infants baptized: who certainly cannot yet believe with the heart to righteousness, or confess with the mouth to salvation, as the thief could; nay, by their crying and noise while the sacrament is administering, they disturb the holy mysteries: and yet no Christian man will say they are baptized to no purpose.

"And if any one do ask for divine authority in this matter: though that which the whole church practises, and which has not been instituted by councils, but was ever in use, is very reasonably believed to be no other than a thing delivered [or ordered] by authority of the apostles."[28]

Augustine (III, *De Anima*) further instructs: "If you wish to be a Catholic, do not believe, nor say, nor teach, that infants who die before baptism can obtain the remission of original sin." And again (Ep. xxviii, *Ad Hieron.*): "Whosoever says that even infants are vivified in Christ when they depart this life without the participation of His Sacrament (Baptism), both opposes the Apostolic preaching and condemns the whole Church which hastens to baptize infants, because it unhesitatingly believes that otherwise they can not possibly be vivified in Christ."

As late as 360, Basil says that "any time of one's life is proper for baptism."[29] This indicates that the custom had not yet crystallized into dogma in his time.

Gregory of Nazianzus (*ca.* 330-*ca.* 390) takes an interesting middle-of-the-road position, in which he apparently tries to preserve features of both infant and adult baptism:

"What say you to those that are as yet infants, and not in capacity to be sensible either of the grace or the miss of it? Shall we baptize them too? Yes, by all means, if any danger make it requisite. . . . As for others, I give my opinion that they should stay three years or thereabouts, when they are capable to hear and answer some of the holy words: and though they do not perfectly understand them, yet they form them. . . . For though they are not liable to give account of their life before their reason be come to maturity, . . . yet by reason of those sudden and unexpected assaults of dangers that are by no endeavour to be prevented, it is by all means advisable that they be secured by the laver [of baptism]."[30]

In his *Christian Archaeology,* Bennett comments on the time element in the transition: "From the fourth century the propriety of the baptism of infants was unquestioned, and the practice was not unusual; nevertheless, adult baptism was the more common practice for the first six centuries."[31]

Says Schaff, "No time can be fixed at which it was first introduced."[32]

"We should remember that during the first three centuries, and even in the age of Constantine, *adult* baptism was the rule, and that actual *conversion* of the candidate was required as a condition before administering the sacrament."[33]

John Henry Cardinal Newman admits that "neither in Rome, nor in Africa, was it then imperative on Christian parents, as it is now, to give baptism to their young children."[34]

Baptism of infants was not practiced in Spain until the year 517, when seven bishops met in Gerona, Catelina, and framed ten rules of discipline.

"The fourth is an agreement to baptize Catechumens only at Easter and Pentecost, except in case of sickness. In the fifth the seven subscribers agree in case infants were ill, and would not suck their mother's milk, if they were offered, to baptize them, even though it were the day that they were born. . . .

"This is the first regulation of the baptism of babes, that was made in Europe."[35]

The baptism of infants, with its corollary, salvation through baptism, made necessary further doctrinal innovations. If a babe became a Christian by baptism without his knowledge, should he not later be initiated into the church *with* his consent? Thus "confirmation" had its beginning. As *The Catholic Encyclopedia* explains, "When infant baptism became customary, confirmation was not administered until the child had attained the use of reason."[36]

Another innovation which followed the adoption of infant baptism was the belief in a "limbo." Gregory Nazianzus early explained this belief as follows:

"It will happen, I believe, . . . that those last mentioned [*i.e.,* infants dying without baptism] will neither be admitted by the just judge to the glory of heaven nor condemned to suffer punishment, since, though unsealed [by baptism], they are not wicked. . . . For from the fact that one does not merit punishment it does not follow that he is worthy of being honoured; any more than it follows that one who is not worthy of a certain honour deserves on that account to be punished."[37]

Augustine came to believe that "unbaptized infants share in the common positive misery of the damned."[38]

Another custom advocated and practiced for many years, and still followed in the Eastern Church, is infant Communion. Since babies were believed to be Christians because of baptism, it seemed only proper to admit the children to the table of the Lord. Cyprian (*ca.* 250) tells of forcing a child to drink the cup:

"The little child, . . . turned away its face, compressed its mouth with resisting lips, and refused the cup. Still the deacon persisted, and, although against her efforts, forced on her some of the sacrament of the cup. Then there followed a sobbing and vomiting. In a profaned body and mouth the Eucharist could not remain; the draught sanctified in the blood of the Lord burst forth from the polluted stomach."[39]

This bizarre practice was eventually discarded in the Western Church, and strongly condemned. The Council of Trent (1545) enjoined: "If anyone saith that the communion of the Eucharist is necessary for little children, before they have arrived at years of discretion; let him be anathema."[40]

As the practice of infant baptism became more widespread, the need for sponsors was felt. Since the child could not respond to the questions asked, someone else must respond for him. The sponsor, who came to be known as a godmother or godfather, was thereafter to be responsible for the moral development of the child. The *Canons of Hippolytus* mention those who make responses for little ones,[41] and Tertullian also mentions them.[42]

# Sprinkling and Pouring

## ❦ 5 ❦

Novatian, a pagan of the third century, became very ill. He did not expect to live, and asked for baptism. Too ill to be immersed according to the custom of the church at that time, he was "baptized" by having water poured on his head as he lay on his couch. However, Novatian did not die as expected. The bishop ruled that the baptism was invalid, and refused to confirm him.

Baptism by pouring came to be known as "clinical baptism" because it was first used primarily for those who were sick. For years the church considered as "irregular" a baptism which had been postponed till one was sick. The Council of Neocaesarea (315) decided that "he that is baptized when he is sick ought not to be made a priest, for his faith is not voluntary, but from necessity."[1]

About the first of the second century the *Didache* had advised: "If you have no running water, baptize in any other; and, if you cannot in cold water, then in warm. But, if the one is lacking, pour the other three times on the head 'in the name of the Father, and Son, and Holy Spirit."[2]

Gregory of Nyssa (*ca.* 331-*ca.* 396) said, "By having the water thrice poured on us and ascending again up from the water, we enact that saving burial and resurrection which took place on the third day."[3]

This innovation in the baptismal ceremony did not come into general use in the Eastern Church. "The Western Church alone adopted as a general rule the practice of sprinkling. This form no doubt became common with the baptism of infants, for all the special provisions in case of bodily weakness would apply to them. We see from the sculptures on many sarcophagi that the practice of sprinkling was frequent at the close of the third century, although the older mode as yet prevailed."[4]

Cyprian was the bishop of Carthage from 248 to 258. In his *Epistle* he allows sprinkling, and thus becomes the first Church Father of whom we have record to give his approval to this type of baptism:

"You have asked also . . . what I thought of those who obtain God's grace in sickness and weakness, whether they are to be accounted legitimate Christians, for that they are not washed, but sprinkled, with the saving water. . . . It appears that the sprinkling also of water prevails equally with the washing of salvation."[5]

The gradual change from immersion to infusion seems to have come about as a matter of convenience. The late Cardinal Gibbons, in his popular *Faith of Our Fathers,* frankly states: "For several centuries after the establishment of Christianity Baptism was *usually* conferred by immersion; but since the twelfth century the practice of baptising by infusion has prevailed in the Catholic Church, as this manner is attended with less inconvenience than Baptism by immersion.

"To prove that Baptism by infusion or by sprinkling is as legitimate as by immersion, it is only necessary to observe that, though immersion was the more common practice in the Primitive Church, the Sacrament was frequently administered even then by infusion and aspersion."[6]

The apologist Pamelius (1536) has written: "Whenever the sick, by reason of their illness, could not be immersed or plunged (which, properly speaking, is to be baptized), they had the saving water poured upon them, or were sprinkled with it. For the same reason I think the custom of sprinkling began to be observed by the Western (Catholic) church, namely, on account of the tenderness of infants, seeing the baptism of adults was now very seldom practiced."[7]

Eventually this form of baptism came into popular use, not only among the ill but also among those in ordinary health. "France seems to have been the first country in the world where baptism by affusion was used ordinarily to persons in health, and in the public way of administering it."[8]

Says Robinson: "It is commonly said, by such as allow immersion to have been the primitive mode of baptism, that dipping was exchanged for sprinkling on account of the coldness of the climates of some countries in connection with the Roman church. Here are two mistakes, the one that dipping was exchanged for sprinkling by choice: and the other that coldness of climate was the reason. It is not true that dipping was exchanged for sprinkling by choice before the reformation, for till after that period the ordinary baptism was trine immersion, and sprinkling was held valid only in cases of necessity."[9]

In Scotland sprinkling was never practiced until after the Reformation, about the year 1550. From there it came south into England during the reign of Queen Elizabeth, but it was not authorized by the Established Church.[10]

The origins of sprinkling as a form of baptism can be traced to ancient primitive rites. The church historian Sozomen records that in the time of Emperor Valentinian (321-375), "when they were about to enter the temple, the priest, in accordance with the pagan custom, sprinkled water upon them with the branch of a tree."[11]

"The sprinkling of children," says Robinson, "is an article of pagan mythology, and it is traced by antiquaries from monument to monument on Roman and Etruscan remains till it hides itself in the most remote antiquity. Among the Pagans, it was lustration: when it first appeared in the church it was under the name of exorcism: when the monks united exorcism with baptism it became confounded with baptism itself: and in the end it came forward, and supplied the place of it."[12]

Mithraic ceremonies made use of "a priest, a godfather, a subject of baptism, an aspersion, an initiation, an initiation to mysteries too, nearly a complete Catholick baptism."[13]

Tertullian noticed these sprinkling lustrations of the pagans. He says that "by carrying water around, and sprinkling it, they everywhere expiate country-seats, houses, temples, and whole cities."[14] Diogenes, as he saw a pagan undergoing such a heathen lustration by aspersion, sneered, "Poor wretch! do you not see that, since these sprinklings cannot repair your grammatical errors they cannot repair either the faults of your life?"[15] Franz Cumont says that Mithra had "a simple sprinkling of holy water."[16]

Virgil says, "Spargens roe levi, et ramo felicis olivae / Lustravitque viros." ("Sprinkling the men with the light spray and a branch of the prolific olive.")[17] Again he is quoted as saying that "when sacred rites were performed to the inferiour deities, a sprinkling sufficed."[18] Pliny[19] and Ovid[20] again speak of the sprinkling used in pagan rites.

One of the heathen fonts is thus described by Angus: "In the Hall of Initiation of the temple of Mên at Pisidian Antioch there was found an oblong depression, of which the most obvious explanation is that it was *lacus* for baptism, not by bathing or immersion, as at Eleusis, but slighter. In the underground pagan shrine, . . . on the via Salaria, the most striking feature is a tank sunk deep in the floor which may well have served as a baptistery in some Mystery-religion."[21]

Among the ancient Romans sprinkling was common. "The bystanders at a funeral removed all pollution which they had incurred, by sprinkling themselves with water."[22] Franz Cumont speaks of the pagan who washed himself in consecrated water, or "sprinkled himself with or drank the blood" of a victim.[23]

Sprinkling has never entirely displaced immersion in the Roman Catholic Church, nor has trine baptism completely disappeared. The Catechism of Pius V states that all forms are acceptable. In the English translation by the Very Rev. J. Donovan, Question XVII asks, "How the Ablution should be made in this mystery of Regeneration." The answer, as decreed at Trent:

"There are three ways of administering baptism, [immersion, effusion, and aspersion]; for those who ought to be initiated by means of sacrament are either immersed into the water, or the water is poured on them, or they are sprinkled with the water. Whichever of these rites is observed, we must believe that the baptism is truly administered; for, water is used in baptism to signify the ablution of the soul, which it accomplishes. . . . Ablution is not more really accomplished by the immersion of any one in water, which we find to have been long observed in the Church from the earliest times, than by the effusion of water, which we now perceive to be the common practice, or by aspersion."[24]

Question XVIII asks whether a single or threefold baptism should be administered, and the answer is given:

"But whether the ablution be performed once or thrice must be held to make no difference; for that baptism was formerly, and may now be, validly administered in the Church in either way, sufficiently appears from the epistle of St. Gregory the Great to Leander. That rite, however, which each individual finds observed in his own church, is to be retained by the faithful."[25]

A later catechism (1949) reads: "The sacrament of Baptism may be validly administered: *first,* by immersion; *second,* by pouring; *third,* by sprinkling."[26]

# Immersion the Age-Old Method of Baptism

### ✿ 6 ✿

Though trine immersion was an early innovation in the baptismal ceremony, there was no question regarding immersion itself. It is true that infant baptism was gradually adopted from the third century on, notwithstanding Tertullian's objections to it. But it was baptism by immersion that was administered to the children.

Only after Christians came to attribute magical properities to the water, and saving virtue to the act itself, did they admit clinical baptism. It was reasoned that if a person could not be saved without baptism, and one who was dying could not be immersed, then a modified form of baptism should be arranged. Eventually the new form was permitted also to persons in health, but it was never accepted universally.

No known council ever enacted a canon condemning baptism by immersion, nor has any pope condemned it. Immersion continued to be the most common and accepted form of baptism for 1,300 years.

"In the primitive Church, and down to the fourteenth century, the ordinary mode of baptism was by immersion of the whole body in water. The original term *baptizo* conveys the meaning of immersion, and no other. On this point we have most valuable testimony from the Fathers of the Church, and other ecclesiastical writers. They invariably designate baptism as the act of *dipping, bathing,* or *washing.*"[1]

Thanks John

Testimony to this fact is abundant in the early writings of the church.

The Pastor (Shepherd) of Hermas, early second century: "They descended with them into the water, and again ascended."[2]

Justin Martyr, *ca.* 150: "They then receive the washing with water."[3]

Tertullian, *ca.* 160-*ca.* 230: "We are immersed."[4]

Hippolytus, *ca.* 220: "He comes up from the baptism."[5]

Porphyry, *ca.* 232-*ca.* 305: "We must feel amazed and concerned about our souls, if a man thus shamed and polluted is to stand out clean after a single immersion."[6]

Cyril of Jerusalem, *ca.* 315-386: "You are about to descend into the baptistery in order to be plunged in water. . . . For he who is plunged in water is surrounded on all sides by water."[7]

Basil, *ca.* 329-*ca.* 379: "How are we to go down with him into the grave? By imitating the *burial* of Christ in baptism; for the bodies of the baptized are in a sense buried in water. . . . By *three immersions,* therefore, and by three invocations we administer the important ceremony of baptism, that death may be represented in a figure."[8]

Ambrose of Milan, *ca.* 340-397: "Thou wast immerged in water, that is, buried."[9] "Ambrosians boast that their baptism is always by immersion."[10]

Augustine, 354-430: "After you professed your belief, three times did we submerge . . . your heads in the sacred fountain."[11]

Zeno, Bishop of Verona during the years 362-380: "You are immersed naked in the font."[12]

Gregory, Bishop of Nyssa, *ca.* 331-*ca.* 396: "We in receiving Baptism, in imitation of our Lord and Teacher and Guide, are not indeed buried in the earth, . . . but coming to the element akin to earth, to water, we conceal ourselves in that as the Saviour did in the earth."[13]

When in 496 Clovis, king of the Franks, was baptized, a contemporary cleric described him as "having entered the life-giving fountain."[14] Alcuin said that Clovis was "washed in the living fountain."[15]

The *Constitutions of the Egyptian Church* (third century) reveal that infants were first dipped in the baptismal font. The word employed, however, does not describe newborn infants, "but designates generally the period of childhood, embracing many years."[16]

The Council of Celchyth, Canterbury, England, 816, made the following pronouncement: "Let ministers take notice that when they administer the holy baptism, that they do not pour the holy water upon the heads of the infants, but that they be always immersed in the font; as the Son of God has in His own person given an example to every believer, when He was thrice immersed into the waters of Jordan. In this manner it ought to be observed."[17]

In Iceland, in the year 984, some refused baptism because they said, "It would be indecent to go naked into the water like little boys to receive baptism, which according to the custom of these times, could only be done by submersion."[18]

St. Bonaventura, 1221-1274, recommended that the way of dipping into the water is "the more common, and the fitter, and the safer."[19]

The great Roman Catholic theologian Thomas Aquinas (*ca.* 1221-1274) stated that "baptism may be given not only by immersion, but also by affusion of water, or sprinkling with it. But it is the safer way to baptize by immersion, because that is the most common custom."[20]

Immersion was originally practiced in the church in Ireland. In his biography of St. Patrick, Rev. Michael J. O'Farrell mentions that in St. Patrick's time "the convert saw in the baptismal fount where he was immersed, the sacred well at which his fathers had worshipped."[21] Pouring and sprinkling were still the exception rather than the rule in the ninth century, according to Walafrid Strabo, but these forms were gradually adopted as the most convenient method as the custom of infant baptism gradually spread.[22]

In 1589 an English writer, Edward Waight, described a baptism he witnessed in Ireland, as follows:

"Their manner of baptizing differeth something from ours; part of the service belonging thereto is repeated in Latin, and part in Irish. The minister taketh the child in his hands, and first dippeth it backwards, and then forwards, over head and ears into the cold water, in the midst of winter, whereby also may appear their natural hardiness."[23]

John Calvin, though he declared that the exact mode of baptism was of little importance, nevertheless commented as follows on the meaning of the term: "The very word *baptize,* however, signifies to immerse; and it is certain that immersion was the practice of the ancient Church."[24]

In pre-Reformation Scotland, "the first law for sprinkling was obtained in the following manner: Pope Stephen II, being driven from Rome by Adolphus, King of Lombards, in 753, fled to Pepin, who, a short time before, had usurped the crown of France. While he remained there the Monks of Cressy, in Brittany, consulted him whether, in case of necessity, baptism poured on the head of the infant would be lawful. Stephen replied that it would, yet pouring and sprinkling was not allowed except in cases of necessity.

"It was not till the year 1311 that the legislature, in a council held at Ravenna, declared immersion or sprinkling to be indifferent.

"In Scotland, however, sprinkling was never practiced, in ordinary cases, till after the Reformation—about the middle of the 16th century.

"From Scotland it made its way into England, in the reign of Elizabeth, but was not authorized in the Established Church."[25]

"In this country, however, *sprinkling was never used in ordinary cases till after the Reformation.* During the persecution of Mary, many persons, most of whom were Scotsmen, fled from England to Geneva, and there greedily imbibed the opinions of that Church. In 1556, a book was published at that place, containing 'The Forms of Prayer, and Ministration of the Sacraments, approved by the famous and godly learned man, John Calvin,' in which the administrator is enjoined to 'take water in his hand, and lay it upon the child's forehead.' These Scottish exiles, who had renounced the authority of the pope, implicitly acknowledged the authority of Calvin; and returning to their own country, with Knox at their head, established sprinkling in Scotland."[26]

Martin Luther's comments regarding baptism by immersion are revealing.

"On this account (as a symbol of death and resurrection), I could wish that such as are to be baptized should be completely immersed into the water, according to the meaning of the word, and to the significance of the ordinance, not because I think it necessary, but because it would be beautiful to have a full and perfect sign of so perfect a thing; as also, without doubt, it was instituted by Christ."[27]

"If you consider what baptism signifies, you will see that the same thing [immersion] is required. For this signifies, that the old man, and our sinful nature, which consists of flesh and blood, is all submerged by divine grace, as we shall more fully show. The mode of baptizing ought, therefore, to correspond to the signification of baptism, so as to set forth a sure and full sign of it."[28]

"Then also without doubt, in German tongues, the little word 'Tauf' [baptism] comes from the word 'tief' [deep], because what one baptizes he sinks deep into the water."[29]

Dr. Philip Schaff says that "Luther sought to restore immersion, but without effect."[30]

When the anabaptists from Zwickau pressed the matter, Melanchthon, Luther's associate, wrote to the elector, declaring "that Satan had attacked them in a weak place, for he knew not how he should refute those enthusiasts: he thought it best not to dispute on this subject, since this article was not of vital importance."[31]

One of the fascinating events in the story of immersion took place in England, where immersion was the common form of baptism until Cromwell's time. In 1644 a group of ecclesiastics gathered to study the form of baptism. Dr. John Lightfoot thus describes the meeting:

"Wed. Aug. 7. This morning we met again. . . . Then fell we upon the work of the day; which was about baptizing of the child, whether to dip him or sprinkle, and this proposition, 'Is it lawful and sufficient to sprinkle this child'—had been canvassed before our adjourning, and was ready now to vote: but I spake against it, as being very unfit to vote, that it is lawful to sprinkle when everyone grants it. Whereupon, it was fallen upon, sprinkling being granted, whether dipping should be tolerated with it. And here fell we upon a large and long discourse, whether dipping were essential or used in the first institution, or in the Jews' custom. . . . After a long dispute, it was at last put to the question, whether the Directory should run thus: The minister shall take water, and sprinkle or pour it with his hand upon the face or forehead of the child: and it was voted so indifferently, that we were glad to count names twice, for so many were unwilling to have dipping excluded, that the votes came to an equality within one; for the one side was twenty-four —and the other, twenty-five: the twenty-four for the reserving of dipping, and the twenty-five against it; and there grew a great heat upon it."[32]

It came up for rediscussion the next day, but "as for the dispute itself about dipping, it was thought fit and most safe to let it alone."[33] So Presbyterians do not immerse, because the decision was lost by one vote!

When John Wesley was forty years of age, he prepared a statement in his own handwriting, which reads as follows: "I believe [myself] it is a duty to observe, so far as I can . . . to baptize by immersion."[34]

A biographer has written of Wesley, "He chose to do it by trine immersion, if the person would submit to it, judging this to be the apostolic method of baptizing."[35] "He would go on baptizing babies by trine immersion, as though his life hung on it." "No baby dare show its face for baptism unless prepared to endure trine immersion."[36]

In Wesley's *Journal* he wrote that "Mary Welsh, aged eleven days, was baptized, according to the custom of the first church and the rule of the Church of England, by immersion. The child was ill then, but recovered from that hour." On May 5 he refused to baptize a child whose parents would not admit immersion.[37]

In his *Explanatory Notes Upon the New Testament,* on Romans 6:4, he says, " '*We are buried with him,*'—Alluding to the ancient practice of baptizing by immersion."[38]

John Telford asserts that Wesley "insisted on baptism by immersion."[39]

"For the first thirteen centuries the almost universal practice of Baptism was that of which we read in the New Testament, and which is the very meaning of the word 'baptize'—that those who were baptized were plunged, submerged, immersed into the water. That practice is still, as we have seen, continued in Eastern Churches. In the Western Church it still lingers [1881] amongst Roman Catholics in the solitary instance of the cathedral of Milan."[40]

"It is a great mistake to suppose that baptism by immersion was discontinued when infant baptism became generally prevalent: the practice of immersion continued even until the thirteenth or fourteenth century. Indeed, it has never been formally abandoned; but is still the mode of administering infant baptism in the Greek church and in several of the Eastern churches. . . .

"After the lapse of several centuries this form of baptism [sprinkling] gradually took the place of immersion, without any established rule of the church or formal renunciation of the rite of immersion."[41]

The earliest known depiction of the baptism of
Christ, from a fresco in the Catacomb of St. Calixtus, Rome. A dove appears at upper left, as Jesus
ascends from the waters of Jordan assisted by John
the Baptist. Second century A.D.

*43*

Representation of a baptism, apparently of a child (though not of an infant), from a fresco in the Catacomb of St. Calixtus, Rome. Dates from early third century A.D. In the painting are light-blue lines around the child. These may suggest baptism by immersion, or they may indicate a pouring of water over the candidate as he stands in the water. In his *On Baptism*, Tertullian says the latter form was commonly used early in the third century.

The baptism of Christ, from a fresco in
the Catacomb of San Ponziano in Rome.

Baptistery in the Catacomb of San Ponziano, Rome.

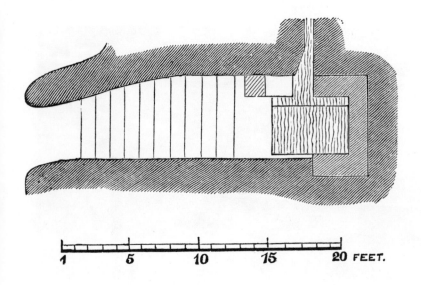

Plan of baptistery in Catacomb of San Ponziano, Rome,
as it would be seen from above.

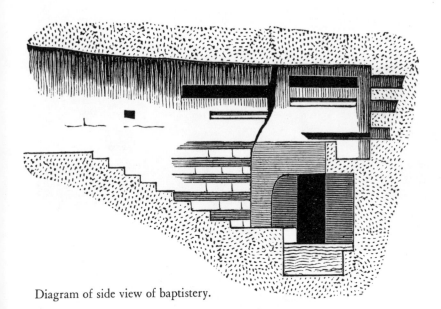

Diagram of side view of baptistery.

47

Ancient Roman bathtubs have been used as Christian baptismal fonts, and still are so used in a few places. Above: tub in Angers Cathedral, France. Below: the tub in Metz.

Baptistery in the early Christian church at Gerasa, Jordan. Gerasa, now known as Jerash, was one of the Ten Cities, or Decapolis, a federation of Greco-Roman cities mentioned in the New Testament.

Baptistery of the Christian basilica at Ephesus.

Baptismal pool in the ruins of the Church of the Virgin Mary, Ephesus.

Quipedib; super ac ambulauia: & aclohacnn& Inlosso
Inae bapazacaus Esa;

The baptism of Christ, as pictured in a manuscript in La Minerva library, Rome.

The baptism of Christ, from a manuscript in the library of the British Museum, *ca.* 1150.

51

Ruins of Cathedral of
St. John at Tyre.

Section of baptistery at
the Cathedral.

Plan of the baptistery.
Maximum depth: three
feet. Dimensions at bot-
tom: 43 by 36 inches.

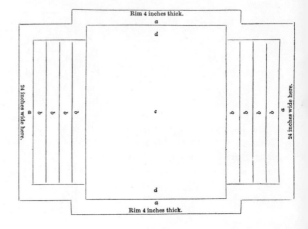

Fourth-century baptistery in Poitiers, France. This is believed to be the oldest extant Christian monument of the Gauls.

Baptistery in the Church of San
Giovanni, Ravenna, Italy, dating
from the fifth century, shows a
recent adaptation from piscina to
small font used for sprinkling.

Fifth-century mosaic depiction of the baptism of Christ, in the dome above the baptistery of the Church of San Giovanni, Ravenna. Both baptistery and picture reveal that the manner of baptism used at that time was as follows: The candidate stood up to his waist in water, as the priest poured water over his head.

*55*

Another fifth-century depiction of the baptism of Christ. This one is found in the Church of Santa Maria de Cosmedin, in Ravenna.

Baptistery in the Church of St. Peter in Terrasa, near Barcelona, Spain, dating from sixth century. It is eight feet long.

Sixth-century baptistery in the Basilica di S. Giusto, Trieste.

Baptistery of the Chiesa dei Pagani in
Aquileja, Italy, from the eleventh century.

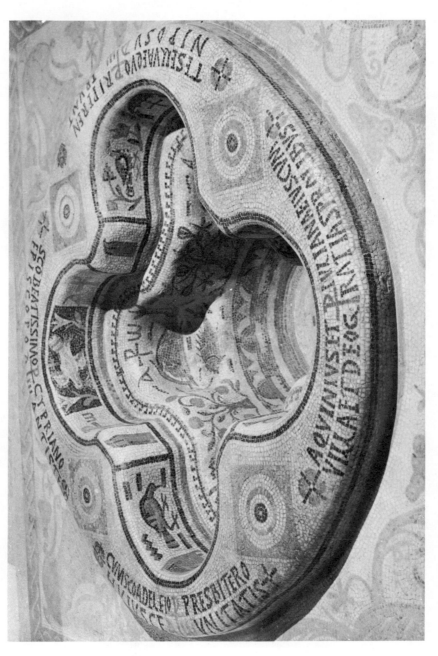

Well-preserved tile baptistery in Kelibia, Tunisia.

5—B.T.C.

Baptismal font in Florence, Italy,
dates from the twelfth century.

Relief of baptism of Jesus by John the Baptist, from a silver altar in the Museo dell' Opera del Duomo, Florence, Italy.

Thirteenth-century mosaic depiction of Christ's baptism, Florence.

Baptistery in the Basilica of St. Mark, Venice, dating
from about the twelfth century. The present baptistery
appears to have been adapted from a larger one used
in earlier centuries, as the mode of baptism changed.

The baptism of Jesus, as depicted in the baptistery at Venice.

Twelfth-century marble baptistery in the Church of San
Frediano, Lucca, Italy, used for baptism by immersion.

Twelfth-century baptistery at Padova, Italy.

Scenes from the life of John the Baptist, in-
cluding the baptism of Christ, at left. (The
head of Christ, submerged in the waters di-
rectly below the dove, has been defaced.)
This relief, appearing on an architrave in the
city of Pisa, dates from the twelfth century.

Baptistery at Parma, Italy, built
during the thirteenth century.

Fourteenth-century Saxon depiction of infant baptism.

In Massa Marittima, Grosseto Province, Italy, this baptismal font is found in the cathedral. The pool below appears to have been used for baptism of adults. The smaller one above was apparently for trine immersions, and the upper one for infant baptism as practiced today. Notice depiction of the baptism of Christ by John the Baptist, in center relief.

Ornate bronze baptistery in the Basilica of St. Peters, Rome. It stands in a depression in the floor, once used for an earlier form of baptism.

In Volterra, Italy, is found this adaptation.

Baptistery in Siena, Italy. This is a
restoration, but three phases of the
history of baptism may still be seen.

Scene in the cathedral of Messina, Sicily, before the earthquake of 1908. Three types of baptism are in evidence.

Symbolic portrayal of infant baptism—modern Italy.

Seventh-day Adventist baptismal service held in 1936 in Hotin, western Romania (now inside Russian border).

# The Monuments Witness to Baptism

### ❧ 7 ❧

It is possible to trace changing attitudes toward baptism through the centuries by examining corresponding changes in baptismal fonts. Ancient churches and ruins in North Africa, Italy, France, and other countries still give their witness.

Baptism was administered by John in the Jordan River; also at Aenon, near Salim, "because there was much water there." John 3:23. The rite was performed in a pond by a desert road (Acts 8:36-39), and, possibly, in a Roman bath in the Philippian jailer's home (Acts 16:33). Later, running water was recommended by the *Didache,* in chapter 7. Justin Martyr says simply that candidates were taken to some place where there was water.[1] Attributed to Clement of Rome is the statement that baptism was performed in a flowing river, in a fountain, or in the sea.[2] Cyprian was baptized in what he called the "birth-giving water," probably on the beach of his beautiful Mediterranean Sea.[3] Tertullian said it made no difference whether one was baptized "in a sea or a pool, a stream or a fount, a lake or a trough," the river Jordan, or the Tiber.[4]

As Christian emissaries penetrated the Roman world, baptisms came to be celebrated in Roman baths. "Rooms of this type were constructed by the Romans as adjuncts to palaces, but more commonly as bath rooms and mausoleums. The Christians employed them for the same purposes, that is, as mausoleums and baptisteries. . . .

"Though such buildings were never constructed for use as churches, they were obviously very appropriate as baptisteries. The baptistery was essentially a bath room, and it naturally assumed the shape which was common for public and private baths among the Romans. The pool or basin occupied the centre, and there was sufficient room about it to accommodate the candidates, with their sponsors and the clergy; baptism, being essentially a personal and private sacrament, did not require the presence of the congregation. . . . Among the Romans the pool was commonly octagonal, and this became the almost invariable tradition in the Church. S. Ambrose attempted to attach a symbolical significance to the octagonal form; and the fact that this form has been perpetuated in the mediaeval (and modern) fonts is perhaps to be traced back ultimately to the Roman bath."[5]

Early baptisteries are found in the catacombs, where by the flickering light of hundreds of candles men were buried in the baptismal waters. "The oldest western fonts are found in the Roman catacombs, cisterns hewn from the tufa in the floor of baptismal chapels. Examples are to be found in the Ostrian Cemetery, where in a small shallow basin in the floor a spring wells up[;] in the Cemetery of Pontianus, where an oblong reservoir, about eighteen square feet in surface area and three feet in depth, is yet filled with water; . . . and of St. Priscilla, where in 1901 was found a basin of particular interest on account of its presumably high antiquity as a baptismal centre."[6] (However, some authorities question whether any baptisms were conducted in the catacombs.)

After Constantine's Edict of Milan, granting liberty to the Christians, commodious churches were built, and by the side of many of these separate baptisteries were erected. Each had a piscina for the immersion of candidates. "These places formed an edifice separate but contiguous to the churches. And as the days on which baptism was administered were few and the number of illuminated ones was great, therefore these baptisteries had to be large and spacious. . . . Ordinarily in each baptistery there were two conclaves, or habitations, that could be closed, one for men and one for women. In the middle was located a font or receptacle for water, called many times the *piscina* [the trough, or, literally, the "fishpond"], ordinarily circular in form, in which the candidates were submerged. The water came to this piscina [or fishpond] by means of canals. . . . After the sixth century the baptisteries began to be placed inside the church; and after the rite of immersion was no longer used, a new form was taken up in many places, which was very different from the ancient rite. . . .

"Regarding the shape and adornments of the baptisteries, although there is some uncertainty, nevertheless Fleury, supported by Anastasius, Gregory of Tours, and Durandus, says the following: 'The baptistery was ordinarily round, with a basin into which descent was made by stairs to enter into the water. It was properly a bath, which was later reduced in size to one large marble or porphyry receptacle, and finally to that of the font as used at present.' "[7]

The historian Baronius tells of a little boy in Rome, A.D. 384, who broke through the crowd watching a baptism in one of the early baptisteries. The unfortunate lad fell into the water and was drowned.[8] This indicates something of the size of the piscina.

The construction of old baptisteries found in Europe and the Middle East testifies to a gradual evolution in the form of administering baptism. First, there was total immersion of the adult catechumen. Then, after Christianity had progressed to the place where most of the adults had already been Christianized, the children were accepted for baptism. The fonts then were made smaller, and used for the immersing of smaller candidates.

Eventually sprinkling was introduced, and the churches built from the seventh century onward usually have small fonts.

*The Catholic Encyclopedia* bears witness to the gradual disappearance of immersion:

"Immersion gradually gave way to infusion, though in the South the custom of immersing children in the baptisteries persisted long after the North had commenced infusion."[9]

"The passing of the period of adult conversion to Christianity and the growing prevalence of infant baptism with a consequent frequency of administration determined a change in the structure of the fonts. Instead of a basin below the floor level, walls of masonary were built up to a height of three or four feet, to facilitate the ministers holding a child over its opening; or a font hewn from solid stone rested on the chapel floor. Immersion of children had come to be the rule, and as the practice was adopted too in the case of adults, the fonts were sometimes large enough to admit of their being immersed. With the thirteenth century, however, simple infusion came by degrees to be adopted, and with its general use, the font became smaller and more shallow, and was raised from the floor on piers or columns."[10]

## Baptisteries in North Africa

The baptismal font in Timgad, North Africa, is one of the most beautiful in existence. It is octagonal, and paved with colored half-inch-square stone tiles. In size it is adequate for the immersion of the largest adult.

Near the site of ancient Carthage are found the ruins of St. Cyprian's basilica. Its ancient font for immersion still exists as a witness to the method of baptism followed in Cyprian's time.

According to Hatchett's *Guide,* at Announa, Algeria, "a baptismal piscina is noticed."[11] At Tebessa, Algeria, there is a baptistery; "the piscina in which the neophites descended is a circular basin, surrounded by steps."[12] At Carthage, near Tunis, "there in a great hall, divided into several sections, was a baptistery of hexagonal form."[13] In the museum at Tunis there is a small baptismal font that could have been used only for immersing an infant. At Sbeitla, Tunis, is "a baptistery with a baptismal basin entirely paved with mosaics."[14]

At Djemila, Algeria, is "a magnificent covered baptistery of round form supported by four columns, which rest upon the corners of a square piscina, around the piscina two circular galleries, entirely paved by beautiful mosaics."[15] At Tipaza "one of the halls contains a round baptismal font, surrounded by steps."[16]

## Baptisteries in the Balkans

In Adam Klissi, on the Black Sea in Romania, are found the ruins of an ancient church with its ancient baptismal font. At Salona, near Split, on the Dalmatian Coast, is another fine baptistery. This is in the ruins of the old city to which Diocletian retired after his abdication. Another old baptistery is found at San Donato, Zadar, Yugoslavia, and in the Basilica of S. Giusto in Trieste is a remarkable baptismal font for the immersion of children. This dates from the sixth century.

## Middle Eastern Baptisteries

The Coptic church in Old Cairo, Egypt, has a fine baptistery. This was the church of St. Sergius and St. Bacchus. "In the narthex we came to a space in the floor which was boarded over. He lifted a plank and exposed an enormous baptismal font, like a small swimming-bath. Coptic baptism is by total immersion, and in the early days, when the Church gained adult converts, they entered this tank of water together, but now the tanks are rarely used."[17]

The church of St. Menas in Egypt once had a baptistery, of which Finegan writes: "A monumental baptistery church was erected at the western end of the first church. . . . In the center of its marble pavement was the deep marble tank, entered by steps from each side, in which the immersions were conducted."[18]

This baptistery was constructed about the end of the fourth century. It is about five feet deep and twenty feet long.

The same author tells of the church of St. Babylas at Kaloussie, in which the baptistery "was large enough to receive the candidate into the water but not large enough to provide for his immersion."[19] The ceremony, therefore, must have been carried out by affusion.

The ruins of an old church, probably dating from the early part of the fourth century, are found on the site of the ancient city of Tyre. Near it are the ruins of a baptistery which was cut from a solid block of white marble. A visitor to this site has described it thus:

"We stood beside a marble structure, close to the wall, evidently as old as the church, and an original part of it. I took my tape-measure and noted the dimensions. . . . There are four steps at either end. . . . The extreme length, inside, is five feet and six inches. The depth is three feet. The width three feet and seven inches. Professor Sepp [the German excavator] said, 'They immersed people here. . . .

"They only baptized the grown people then.' "[20]

The baptistery built in early times at St. Sophia, in Constantinople, still stands. The baptistery is "very large, and councils have been held in it, and it was called . . . the great Illuminatory. In the middle was the bath, in which baptism was administered, it was supplied by pipes, and there were outer rooms for all concerned in the baptism of immersion, the only baptism of the place."[21]

## Baptisteries in Italy

In Italy a wealth of monumental evidence to changing baptismal practices may still be seen. The font of the Basilica of St. John in the Lateran, Rome, supposedly donated by Constantine in the fourth century, is a thing of beauty. The edifice is octagonal, and the roof is supported by huge columns. Within a circular wall around the baptistery are seen the three phases of the evolution of the font as the mode of baptism evolved from adult immersion to pouring. Once the font was below the level of the floor, but in time this was filled and then a beautiful bath was erected for the baptism of children. This is no longer used, but above it now is a receptacle for the pouring of children.

This progression is also seen in many other fonts. In the cathedral of Massa-Marittima in the province of Grosseto there is a small baptismal font superimposed over a larger one which undoubtedly rests on the original piscina of ancient times. The upper one dates from about the fourteenth century.

Two fonts may be seen in Parma. One is a gigantic stone circular bowl, fully four feet in diameter, resting on a lion. The other is an octagonal font which has since been filled, with a smaller well allowed to remain in the center. These both date from the thirteenth century. The original is eight feet in diameter and four feet deep. In an official report forwarded to the pope on November 21, 1578, description of the baptistery and its uses was given. The manner of baptism was described as *"Baptizant per immersionem."*

"In one corner of the baptistery is a smaller font. . . . All the children born in Parma are now brought to this font to be sprinkled, a practice which was introduced after the seventeenth century, and mentioned for the first time in 1622."[22]

There are two fonts in Siena. The more modern portion of the one dating from the eleventh century, in the church of San Giovanni, is hexagonal. Like that of Massa-Marittima it has three tiers. The latest, of quite recent construction, is used for sprinkling. It stands in a font formerly used for immersing infants. This in turn appears to be built upon a filled-in piscina. The other font is in the cathedral and is of smaller size.

Only two of the steps in this change are evident in the Basilica of San Marco in Venice. The same incomplete evolution is seen in the font in Orvieto, in the cathedral in Messina, and in the church of Santa Maria Maggiore in Toscanella.

The church of San Giovanni in Fonte in Verona has a large font twenty-eight feet in circumference. Hewn out of one piece of Venetian marble, it is four and a half feet deep. This baptistery dates from the twelfth century.[23] At Cividale, in the province of Venetia, in the duomo dating from 750, there is a baptismal font, as reconstructed in the fifteenth century, four and a half feet in diameter and three feet deep. In Bologna, in the court of the church of San Stefano, is a large marble basin once used as a baptismal font. This dates from about the eighth century.

Sizable fonts may be seen in Cremona, Ascoli, Savona, and Torcello.

In Albenga the baptistery, probably dating from the seventh or eighth century, has steps leading to the font.[24] Pisa has a baptismal font dating from 1153, probably not finished until the fourteenth century. The font is fourteen feet in diameter and four feet deep.

The Pesaro baptistery dates from very early times. The pavement of its hexagonal-shaped font was made of large slabs of Grecian marble. There is in this baptistery a second font, probably used exclusively for women. There are three steps leading down into the basin.

Another superb ancient font is found in Aquileia. Doubtless it was once covered by a baptistery, but today it is protected by a tile roof supported by six columns. The font, of hexagonal form, is thirteen feet wide at the top, but narrows to five feet at the bottom step. The depth is sufficient for a man to stand in the water up to his neck.

In the baptistery of Padua, dating from the twelfth century, is a circular font five feet in diameter and four feet deep built over what appears to be a more ancient piscina. The church of San Agate al Comocchio has a small font built in the large font once used for immersion.

A volume edited by the Touring Club of Lombardy mentions the baptistery of San Satiro in Milan, erected in the ninth century. In Milan also, in the ancient church of San Lorenzo, two baptisteries existed very early: San Giovanni alle Fonti, exclusively for men, and San Stefano alle Fonti, for women. St. Augustine was baptized in this church. The Gothic invasion damaged the baptisteries, but they were restored in the fifth century. The Ambrosian rite, which included immersion, was also performed in the cathedral of Milan.

Also in Milan is an old Ambrosian church containing a baptistery three feet in diameter, in which Ambrose probably baptized children. Under the pulpit is a large sarcophagus which may have been used as a baptismal font.

The church of Pieve de Santa Maria and St. Gregoria in Brancoli has an old font built on a large base which seems to have been an old piscina. The upper one dates from the thirteenth century. A square font is found in Pieve Buggiano Alto.

Ruins of an ancient church in San Stefano, near Rome, were excavated. "On the right . . . is a square baptistery, with a sunken semi-circular font in the centre, evidently for baptism by immersion."[25]

An old Roman bath dating from the fourth century was used as a baptistery in Nocera dei Pagani. It needed no adaptation, as it was sufficiently large for adult immersion.

In the cathedral of Novara is a sepulchral urn that was once used for baptism by immersion. It rests in a basin. "The large basin which contains it, and was undoubtedly the original baptismal font, is octagonal in form, and provided with three steps inside and an outlet for the escape of the water. It is about four feet deep and eight feet wide."[26]

Before the earthquake of 1908, the cathedral of Messina contained a fine example of a new type of baptistery built over the ancient immersion font.

The large font in the church of St. Maria in Castello, Tarquinia, is superimposed on a square base that appears to have been a still larger piscina. It dates from the eleventh century.

At Toscanella the tenth-century baptistery is hexagonal, and superimposed on what appears to be a much larger one. The present one is about three feet in diameter, but the larger one is fully eight feet in diameter.

In Florence the original font, built in 1371, is twelve feet wide and four and one-half feet deep. There were probably several fonts in the building at one time. Ten feet below the present floor of the great baptistery, in the subterranean grotto, is another baptistery. Here are old stone walls comparable to those of ancient Rome. It probably dates from the third or fourth century. The octagonal walls seem to have formed the original baptistery. There is also now a font for sprinkling.

Pistoia has a fine baptistery in San Giovanni Rotondo. The building is octagonal in shape, with a square basin ten feet in diameter and four feet deep. The building dates from 1337.[27]

In Lucca, in the church of San Frediano, the font is circular, about five feet in diameter, and its sides are sculptured with allegorical pictures. It dates from the twelfth century.

A fine baptismal font exists in the church of St. Peter Pieve in Toscana.

The church of San Leonardo in Cerreto Guidi in the province of Venice has a baptismal font dating from the year 1511.

There are two baptisteries in Ravenna. The older, in San Giovanni in Fonte, was a Roman bath which was made into a baptistery in the fifth century. In the center is a large bath ten feet in diameter, three and one-half feet deep. The font has been removed from the other baptistery, which is now a part of the oratory of the church of Santa Maria in Cosmedin.

In the former basilica of St. Peter's in Rome Pope Damasus I (367) erected a basin for immersion. Of this, Cardinal Bullion in his *Historia Templi Vaticani* says, "This basin was large and deep, for the administration of trine immersion, according to the rite of baptism in those times."[28] This font was pulled down with the ancient basilica.

The wonderful baptismal font now used in St. Peter's was formerly the cover of the tomb of Hadrian. It stands in a basin hollowed out in the floor. "Benedictus XIII, elected Pope in 1724, being anxious to conform to the ancient rite of administering baptism by immersion, ordered the construction of two steps below the pavement, forming thus a large basin, in which persons could be immersed with ease. Now that the primitive rite is definitely abandoned, this basin is partly closed with a wooden pavement."[29]

An inscription found there, reads: "Benedict XIII., . . . constructed this font of human regeneration for the ancient rite, in the year of salvation, 1725."[30]

Excavations in Ostia at the mouth of the Tiber during the Mussolini era revealed a small basilica. In it is a baptistery containing a marble tank with water pipes still intact. This is considered by some to be the oldest Christian baptistery in existence today.

Naples has a baptistery erected, it is believed, by Constantine in 303. "A circular pavement of white marble, . . . now covers the space formerly occupied by the baptismal font."[31]

"More or less interesting examples of baptisteries exist at Biella, Brindisi, Cremona, Galliano, near Milan, Gravedona, Monte Sant' Angelo, . . . Pinara, Pistoia, Spalato, Verona, and Volterra."[32]

In Italy there are some sixty-seven baptisteries dating from the fourth century to the fourteenth. Others are mentioned in documents but no longer exist. All bear witness to the gradually changing attitudes toward the baptismal ceremony.

## Baptisteries on the Iberian Peninsula

The Portuguese village of Odrinhas a few miles north of Sintra, the old summer capital of the kings, has a baptistery built in the times of the Visigoths. It is an octagonal stone building. The rear wall, well preserved, is about sixteen feet high. The baptistery is distinctly visible, though the tank itself is filled with rubble.

In Lisbon is an archaeological museum in what was, before the Lisbon earthquake in 1755, an old church. The building contains a baptistery about thirty inches in diameter, sufficiently large for the immersion of infants.

The cathedral in Barcelona, Spain, has an immense metal bowl almost five feet wide. Inside it is a small marble font.

An ancient church in Tarrasa, Spain, still retains its old baptismal font measuring nine by twelve feet. In July, 1927, the municipality printed a pamphlet with descriptions of points of interest in the town. Included is the photograph of this old baptistery of St. Michael, with the explanation that it is a rare work constructed in either the fifth century or the eighth or the ninth. The belief is that it served for baptism by immersion. Three chapels form a crypt that might have been used for tombs of martyrs, or perhaps a font for immersion of women.

Other such baptisteries are found in churches in Toledo and Palma de Mallorca.

## Baptisteries in Germany

In the cathedral of Magdeburg there is a font three feet in diameter and a foot and a half in depth, dating from the fourteenth century.[33]

The church of St. Sebaldus in Nürnburg has a copper baptistery in which King Wenceslaus was baptized as a baby in 1361. It is three feet in diameter, and about twenty inches deep. It has a grate underneath where fire can be kindled to heat the water. "The size of these fonts testifies to immersion as being formerly the common mode of baptism in Germany."[34]

## Baptisteries in Prussia and Austria

Otho, apostle to the Pomeranians, with his assistants baptized 22,000 people at Julin and Stettin.[35] "He ordered the erection of three baptisteries. . . . These baptisteries were great vats sunk into the ground, and surrounded with curtains."[36]

In Salzburg there is a large metal basin five feet wide, dating from the thirteenth century.

The St. Stephens Dom in Vienna has an enormous stone basin six feet wide, dating from 1481.

## Baptisteries in France

The Cluny Museum, Paris, has two metal fonts or tubs about twenty-six inches in diameter and eighteen inches deep, that were used as baptisteries in the fourteenth century. They are large enough for the immersion of infants. One is lead. The other is brass, with an inscription giving its origin: "EMBSEN PIUS LUNEBOURG." It dates from the fourteenth century.

At the cathedral of Metz is a beautiful porphyry baptistery once used as a bathtub by the Romans. It is more than nine feet long and almost five feet wide at the top.

The cathedral of Angers has a baptistery now used as a holy-water font. It is an old Roman bath or sarcophagus of porphyry almost five feet long.

An octagonal building constructed in the twelfth century for a baptistery stands in Le Puy. There is one in Frejus beside the cathedral, there is one in Aix, and there is one at Chalons, also beside the cathedral. Near the old cathedral of Marseilles is a baptistery built in the fifth century.

In Thouveil there is a peculiar font in the form of a trough, four feet in length. Another like it is to be found in the church of Limay, near Nantes.

The church of St. Peter's at Montdidier has a font of the eleventh century. In the Louvre Museum, Paris, is a font brought from the East on the occasion of the baptism of the sons of St. Louis.

Notre Dame of Paris contains a "font remarkable in ecclesiastical history, . . . in which Clovis, the first Catholic, if not the first Christian king of the Franks, was baptized."[37] It is "of polished porphyry, fully seven feet long, about two and a half feet deep, and nearly the same in width."[38]

Notre Dame of Chartres has a stone font the size of a half barrel dating from the twelfth century, in which infants were immersed.

Poitiers has one of the most notable of the ancient baptisteries, dating from the fourth century, when Hilaire was bishop. The following information was copied by Dr. A. J. Girou, a personal friend of the author, from mimeographed sheets on display at the Poitiers baptistery:

"According to archaeological documents, St. John's Baptistery, which was composed of a cello covering a piscina for baptisms by immersion, preceded by a rectangular room accompanied by small rooms, would have been built in the fourth century with fragments of Roman monuments. . . .

"Up to the seventh century it was customary to baptize by immersion in a piscina. The feet of the candidate rested in water.

"This custom being no more practical for worship, toward 680 it was changed into baptism by sprinkling, as it is done today, with a basin placed at the height of the hand which was called a baptismal font.

"It is supposed that toward the seventh century the piscina

would have been filled up and the baptismal font created for baptism by sprinkling, of which a model still exists near the piscina.

"From that time on, the deep piscina, intended for adults, became useless. It disappeared under the pavement, which was raised higher, and the new font rose on the same place. In Christianized Gaul, the new converts were scarce, the custom of baptizing children was generalized. . . . In fixing upon the eighth century, at the latest, the general adoption in the West of baptism by pouring—"

## Baptisteries in Belgium

The Archeological Museum in Brussels exhibits a brass font from Tirlemont dating from the middle of the twelfth century. There is another, of still greater artistic merit, at Liege in the church of St. Bartholomew. It is of bronze, and round, resting on a base surrounded by twelve bulls. This font was made in 1112.[39]

## English Baptisteries

An old English book describes the baptisteries in England as follows:

"As immersion was practiced by the church in this country until the Reformation, and perhaps occasionally later (as will afterwards appear) all Fonts were up to that period made sufficiently large for the purpose. Hence, by a constitution of Edmund Archbishop of Canterbury, A.D. 1236, the Font is directed to be 'competens.' "[40]

"We have stated that until the Reformation, and perhaps occasionally after it, dipping was practised in this country. That pouring or sprinkling were not unusual previous to the Reformation is very probable, for, so early as the year 754, pouring in cases of necessity was declared by Pope Stephen the Third to be lawful [Robinson's *History of Baptism,* p. 429]: and in the year 1311 the council of Ravenna declared dipping or sprinkling indifferent. [*Ibid.,* p. 430.] Yet dipping appears to have been in this country the more usual mode; for from an illumination in Rous's life of Richard Beauchamp Earl of Warwick, who was born in 1381, it appears that the earl was baptized by dipping [Cott. MSS. Julius, E. IV.]; so Prince Arthur (eldest son of Henry VII.) King Edward VI. and Queen Elizabeth were all dipped. [Robinson, *op. cit.*, p. 120; also Harl. MSS. 6079.] Not one of the rituals which we have examined contains any permission to use pouring or sprinkling when the child is brought to the church. The first instance of pouring being allowed in public baptism is in the first prayer book of Edward VI. which says, 'And if the childe be weake, it shall suffice to poure water upon it.' [*Common Prayer*, A.D. 1459, p. 128.] In all probability dipping was from this time, by degrees, abandoned; but many years elapsed ere it was so entirely."[41]

The author, Prowett, then tells of the existence of several old piscinas, or baptisteries, wherein adult baptism was undoubtedly performed.

In Helpringham, Lincolnshire, "in the chancel, the sides of which are Early English, are three very good Early English stalls and a piscina of the same date."[42]

According to the same author, the Threckingham, Lincolnshire, church "contains a piscina and closet apparently of the same period [Early English]."[43] Also, "the chapel of Noseley contains three very good Early English stalls and a double piscina."[44] In Heckington, Lincolnshire, "in the chancel are the most gorgeous stalls and piscina we ever saw."[45] In Horbling, Lincolnshire, "some parts of the chancel are Norman, of which the piscina should be noticed as a Norman piscina is not very commonly seen."[46]

"By an ancient ecclesiastical constitution (A.D. 1236) [*Constitutiones Edmundi,* can. 10] a font of stone was required to be placed in every church, and it was to be capacious enough for total immersion. . . .

" 'In every baptismal church let there be a baptistery of stone, or however, one that is sufficient (large enough for dipping such as are baptized in it).' "[47]

The church of St. Peter, Oxford, had "a very ancient baptismal font," circular, with a circumference of eleven feet and of proportionate depth.[48] Cranbrook and Canterbury have baptisteries.[49]

"In Ifley church, Oxfordshire, . . . there is an Anglo-Saxon font, for total immersion, which was the practice adopted in the first ages of Christianity."[50]

A circular font of great antiquity, nine feet two inches in circumference, is in Malvern. It dates from not later than the twelfth century.[51]

"In 1850 there was a large stone baptistery in the parish church of Bradford, Yorkshire, England. . . . It was a large block of stone *about* twelve feet long, *about* six feet wide, and *about* four feet high. On one side of it there was a cavity the necessary size for the immersion of an adult, and on the other an opening large enough for the immersion of a child of three years old. This block of stone, I was informed, was placed in the church by one of the vicars of Bradford about fifty years ago [about 1830]."[52]

Many old baptismal fonts in England were removed from the churches under the Puritan regime of Cromwell, some of them being destroyed.[53]

Thus the many monuments still in existence witness to the adaptation of the baptisteries to changes in the ceremony itself. At first the baptisteries were large enough for immersion of adults. They became smaller as the candidates knelt in them and were immersed three times forward, or stood in them to have water poured on their heads. Then many were filled up and raised so that a smaller font appears; in these infants were immersed. In some of these were placed still smaller receptacles for the smaller quantity of water needed for pouring or sprinkling.

# Baptism Portrayed in Art

### ❦ 8 ❧

This evolution of the baptismal rite is sketched in crude pictures found in the catacombs, rough sculptures of the early centuries, figured bronze doors, mosaics, and paintings by master artists. Obviously, the artists pictured baptism as they saw it about them; they mirrored the customs of their day.

"The oldest baptismal pictures date, perhaps, from the second century, coming from the most ancient part of the catacomb of St. Calixtus. They all represent the baptized standing in a stream with the administrant on dry ground, the former being nude, the latter more or less clothed. The very oldest picture represents the new convert as 'coming up after immersion from the river which reaches over his knees, and joining hands with the baptizer, who is drest in a tunic and assists him in ascending the shore. . . . As far as they go all of the pictures confirm the river baptism prescribed by the *Didache* as the normal form, in imitation of the typical baptism in the Jordan. . . . From these pictorial representations we have a right to draw the inference that immersion was as complete as the depth of the accessible stream or fount would admit.' "[1]

In the cemetery of Pontianus is a picture of Jesus standing unclothed in waist-deep water, with John the Baptist pouring water over His head.[2]

The fonts themselves, in the decorations about the sculptured

*(91)*

sides, often carried descriptions of baptism. Usually pouring or dipping is portrayed. It must be remembered that trine immersion first entered the church in the second century. A number of pictures of baptism by immersion have been discovered.

"The church adjoining [the baptistery of Aquileia] has a picture of baptism by immersion, which rite was practiced for more than nine centuries."[3]

On the baptismal font of Verona is a picture of the baptism of Christ. "The water of the Jordan is raised into a hillock, and our Saviour is being immersed in it."[4]

The baptistery of Pisa has a baptismal scene of Jesus in the Jordan in water up to His neck.[5]

A scene of Christ in the Jordan is portrayed on the gate of the baptistery of Parma. Both John and the Saviour are standing in the water to the waist. This dates from the thirteenth century.

On the southern door of the baptistery in Florence is a picture of Christ being baptized by John. Jesus is standing waist-deep in water.

"In St. Peter's Church, at Cologne, is a fresco representing the immersion of Rubens, the painter, when an infant, in 1577."[6]

"There are still existing in several churches of France paintings of baptism by immersion. In the cathedral of Sens a painted window contains a representation of the baptism of Eutropus by Simon and Jude. Under the portico of the cathedral of Bourges, Ursinus is shown as baptizing by immersion the son of Leocades, governor of the Gauls. Upon the entrance of the church of St. Trophimus, at Arles, is sculptured a baptismal scene."[7]

On the sides of an old baptistery in Pont de Mousson in France, John the Baptist is represented as baptizing two Jews, who stand in the water up to the waist. On the same font John is shown baptizing the Saviour, who likewise stands in water to the waist.[8]

The church of St. Bridget, Bridekirk, in the county of Cumberland, England, has an ancient font with a rudely sculptured picture of John baptizing Christ.

A font dating from 1150 is exhibited in the Archeological Museum in Brussels. On it appears a representation of the baptism of Christ. He is pictured as a child, half immersed in the Jordan, with John the Baptist standing on His right side and a dove hovering overhead.

In the St. Bartholomew church, Liege, Belgium, is a font on the side of which appears the baptism of Christ. He is standing half immersed in water, with John at His side.

The ancient baptistery of Ravenna has in the cupola a mosaic of the baptism of Christ. In it Jesus stands up to His waist in the water. A similar baptismal scene is found in the baptistery connected with the church of Santa Maria in Cosmedin, Ravenna.

One of the most remarkable sculptures is that on the baptismal font of the cathedral of Massa-Marittima in Toscana, dating from 1267. It pictures John the Baptist baptizing Christ, who stands neck-deep in water. John has his hand on Christ's forehead, and an angel stands on the bank with His clothes.

## Pictures and Mosaics

In addition to the fonts themselves, excellent sculptured scenes of Christ's baptism and some fine mosaics and paintings have been preserved.

"Besides these actual specimens, the font is also depicted in the remains of early Christian art. In nearly every instance it is a shallow pool or basin in which the neophyte stands with feet immersed."[9]

The crypt of the Catacomb of Santa Lucina has an ancient painting (perhaps from the fourth or fifth century) of John the Baptist reaching out his hand to assist Christ, who is standing in the Jordan shoulder deep. The Holy Spirit, in the form of a dove, hovers above.

In the Cappella Palatina of the Palazzo Reale in Palermo, Sicily, the immersion of Christ is pictured in beautiful mosaic, dating from the twelfth century.

## *Manuscripts*

The Vatican Library contains several manuscripts accompanied by pictures of baptism by immersion:

Vatican Codex MS. 1156, a Greek Evangelisterium of the twelfth century: Baptism of Christ.

V. MS. Palatine 871. Latin, Historia Sacra, Baptism of Christ. Fourteenth century.

V. MS. 8541, Acta Sanctorum. Several pictures of baptism by immersion and by affusion, fifteenth century.

V. MS. Palatine 413. Baptism of Christ, fifteenth century.

V. MS. Reginae 99. fol. 24. Baptism of Christ in the Jordan. Underneath are the words, "Flumis baptizam imersione."[10]

The Bibliothèque Nationale, Paris, MS. 94 has a tenth-century Greek Gospel containing ten pictures of baptism by immersion.

In the library of the British Museum is a thirteenth-century document (Harleian, 1527), *Novum testamentum figuris depictis illustratum*. This contains twenty-seven pictures of baptism by immersion.

"In the library of the Duke of Devonshire, there is a manuscript of the tenth century, which contains a picture of the baptism of Christ by immersion."[11]

The Barberini Library at Rome has a Greek Psalter of the eleventh century, in which Philip is pictured baptizing the eunuch. The candidate is in the water to his shoulders, with Philip standing on the bank with his hand on the head of the one to be baptized.[12]

# The Protest
# of the Centuries

## ❧9❧

The gradual abandonment of the simple initiatory rite of church entrance—baptism by immersion—and the adoption of other forms, met with energetic resistance. Some of the opponents of change passed the torch of protest to others. In other cases, "Protestants before the Reformation," as one writer calls them, seemed to spring up spontaneously. Their history is oft-times obscure, their witness many times clouded with heresies. Testimony regarding them has come mostly through the writings of their enemies. "It is a complicated task to determine the true character and the tenets of any ancient sect, considering that almost all the information that has reached us has come from the opponents. The heretical literature has to a great extent either perished or been completely changed; but much has also survived in a modified written form or through oral tradition."[1]

The historian well knows the difficulty of accurately describing these dissenting groups. Says Burnet, "I soon knew which way so many writings had gone; and . . . I could but wonder at their boldness who thus presumed to raze so many records."[2]

### Montanists

Some of the older Montanists, in the latter part of the second century, still cherished memories of the apostle John. Yet they had absorbed Gnostic, Mithraic, and other pagan influences during the intervening time. In that century-long period Christianity had to combat the fiercest pagan opposition. In many ways it was molded by the thought of the day.

The group of believers was large in places, but the early spirit of piety was somewhat cooled, and the worldliness noted by James (chapter 2:1-7) much earlier, became more pronounced.

Then Montanus appeared, preaching separation from the world. For a century or more his followers insisted that they, rather than the larger body of Christians, constituted the true apostolic church. While it is difficult to define their doctrines precisely, it is clear that they protested certain widespread laxities of doctrine and practice. For this reason John Wesley later said of them: "The Montanists, in the second and third centuries, were real scriptural Christians."[3]

These first protesters have had their spiritual descendants from that time to this. "Leading authorities trace the faith of the Montanists down through the centuries until comparatively recent times. It is seen in Novatianism and the Cathari, in Donatism, among the Paulicians and the Waldenses."[4]

Tertullian (160-230) was an ardent Montanist. Tertullian, it will be remembered, strongly counseled deferment of baptism until reason and stability of life would make the rite more meaningful to converts. The Montanists "insisted that those who had 'lapsed' from the true faith should be rebaptized, because they had denied Christ and ought to be baptized anew. On this account they were termed 'Anabaptists,' and some of their principles reappeared in Anabaptism. . . . Infant baptism was not yet a dogma, and we know that it was rejected by the Montanists."[5]

Montanists, however, like the other dissenting sects that followed them, clung to certain heresies. They entertained the belief that baptismal water itself had a supernatural effect on the believer. This belief was shared by the Novatians.

### Cathari, or Novatians

Novatian was among the first, of whom we have specific record, to be baptized by pouring; and his enemies constantly reminded him that his baptism was irregular. Yet "clinical" baptism gradually came to be practiced for the ill, and centuries later pouring or sprinkling replaced the apostolic rite almost entirely.

Nevertheless Novatianism registered earnest protests against the relaxation of church discipline in the third century. Mosheim says that the Novatians "re-baptized such as came over to them from the Catholics."[6] They were called *Cathari,* the pure ones, and although they were far from following New Testament baptismal practices, they are considered to have been among the first of the anabaptists.

During the persecutions of the church under certain Roman emperors, Christians who lacked fortitude yielded their principles. Then, after the danger ceased, most of the backsliders sought reinstatement in the church. Controversy raged in the church as to whether these people should be rebaptized. Some, who considered baptism a sacrament, insisted that the traditores (traitors) could not be accepted again as Christians. The Novatians, however, allowed rebaptism, and were therefore called "anabaptists" or "rebaptizers."

## Donatists

The Donatists, from A.D. 311 onward, insisted on the same procedure. In addition they taught that baptism, to be valid, must be administered by a worthy minister. To be worthy, the minister must have "an unbroken line of ceremonially and morally unblemished administrators of the ordinance back to the apostles."[7]

The Donatists "were a holy people, professing to enjoy regeneration of heart and subsequent purity of heart; insisted that the true Church is composed only of spiritual Christians."[8] It is not clear whether or not they practiced baptism by immersion.

## Paulicians

The Paulicians originated in Armenia about the year 660 and flourished for three or four centuries. Much uncertainty exists regarding their character and teachings, but Dean Stanley calls them "premature Protestants."[9] They believed they had continued in the doctrines of Paul the apostle, hence their name "Paulicians." Here again, most of what is known of them is derived from the writings of their bitter detractors. However, it is known that the Paulicians held that men must first repent and believe, and then ask for baptism when they are sufficiently mature. They baptized by immersion.

## Bogomils and Others

The Bogomils were twelfth-century Christians of Bosnia, Bulgaria, and Armenia. Though again the sources have been tampered with, it seems clear that they rejected infant baptism. This is probably why certain Catholic writers have stated that the Bogomils did not practice baptism. According to Hagenbach, the Bogomils, like the Paulicians and Cathari, opposed infant baptism.[10]

The Bogomils were an energetic, missionary people that spread over a large portion of Europe. Doubtless they were the inspiration of other dissenting groups such as the Albigenses.

"It is exceedingly difficult, however, to form any precise idea of the Albigensian doctrines, as our knowledge of them is derived from their opponents."[11] Whenever the writings of the Albigenses were discovered by persecutors, they were, of course, destroyed. It is believed that the doctrine of the Albigenses originated in the Paulician movement;[12] thus it is likely that many of the beliefs and practices of the two sects were similar. There seems to be some evidence that the Albigenses baptized by immersion and rejected infant baptism.[13] The Waldensian historian Comba says that the Albigenses "rejected all the sacraments except baptism, which they reserved for believers." Naturally this would mean adults.[14]

## Petrobrusians

Peter of Bruys was the founder of the Petrobrusians. About 1120 he began preaching his distinctive beliefs. Here we have "an almost complete return to New Testament doctrine and practice. Our information about these Reformers is derived wholly from their enemies, yet it is of such a nature that its authenticity can scarcely be called in question."[15] Peter was a French priest who, with access to the Bible, demanded the rebaptism of converted people. He soon had a large following, and his cause was aided by Henry of Lusanne's joining him about 1135. According to Peter the Venerable, the Roman Catholic prelate who opposed these two pre-Reformation Reformers, they denied that the children who have not reached the age of intelligence can be saved by the baptism of Christ. "He [Peter of Bruys] held that persons ought not to be baptized till they come to the use of their reason. Thus he rejected infant baptism."[16]

## Waldensians

The Waldensians are another group whose records were largely destroyed. This movement forms, as it were, a chain that unites the earlier groups with the Reformation. Some of them rejected infant baptism. Waldensian missionaries witnessed in much of Europe.

## Anabaptists

In Europe, the anabaptists arose more or less spontaneously, without a well-recognized founder. For centuries any who taught repentance and profession of faith in Christ before receiving baptism, were labeled anabaptists, or rebaptizers. But in the sixteenth century a more well-defined movement arose. "No one can certainly say whether they appeared first in the Netherlands, Germany, or Switzerland, and their leaders were not confined to any one country, and seem to have had no especial connection with each other."[17] They retained baptism in the simple New Testament form and took no special name, but called themselves "Christians" or "Brethren." Their general belief was that Christians should live apart from the world. Their literature was almost nonexistent; little of it has been preserved.

Erasmus wrote of them as Hussites, saying that they "renounce all rites and ceremonies of the Catholic Church; . . . they admit none into their communion until they are dipped in water, or baptized."[18] Their purpose was to restore primitive Christianity as they saw it. Naturally, it was resented energetically by the established church. L'Abbé Fleury, the Roman Catholic historian, wrote of them in 1523:

"This was called the heresy of the Anabaptists, because the name was attributed to this erroneous sect, for they baptized in a sacred fountain all those baptized in infancy, and they condemned baptism given to little children. . . . Neither did they detest baptism the less, and all, as many as gave name to their own faction, dipped again in the sacred fountain; whence they were called Anabaptists."[19]

## Mennonites

Menno Simons was a Roman Catholic priest who left his church and became the recognized leader of the anabaptists of the Low Countries. From him the Mennonites took their name.

Several hundred years later Dr. Ypeij, one of the professors of theology of the Groningen University, and the Rev. J. J. Dermont, chaplain to the king of the Netherlands, were asked to report on the origins of the Mennonites. The report (1819) stated: "The Mennonites are descended from the tolerably pure evangelical Waldenses, who were driven by persecution into various countries; and who during the latter part of the twelfth century fled into Flanders; and into the provinces of Holland and Zealand, where they lived simple and exemplary lives, in the villages as farmers, in the towns by trades, free from the charge of any gross immoralities, and professing the most pure and simple principles, which they exemplified in a holy conversation. They were, therefore, in existence long before the Reformed Church of the Netherlands."[20]

Mosheim writes that *"Mennonites* are not altogether in the wrong, when they boast of a descent from those Waldenses, Petrobrusians, and others, who are usually styled *the Witnesses for the truth* before Luther."[21]

Menno Simons was convinced of the need of rebaptism by reading the New Testament. He was led to this study as he endeavored to discover why in 1531 a man by the name of Sicke Freerks of Frierichs (better known as Snyder), a tailor, was done to death, as the court record says, "because he has been rebaptized and perseveres in that baptism."[22] Simons refused to have any connection with the Münsterites in their violences. He wrote much. In his *Fundamental Book of True Christian Faith,* published in 1539, he maintains "the spiritual idea of the church, as a communion of true saints, and the necessary consequence of this idea, the rejection of infant baptism."[23]

In three centuries Mennonites have scattered through Europe, into Russia, and to the United States, where they are numerous in certain sections. They have maintained to a great extent the witness of strongly evangelical beliefs and sincere Christian lives.

### Baptists

What is known today as the Baptist movement arose in Holland and spread to England. "After 1610 we have an unbroken succession of Baptist churches, established by indubitable documentary evidence."[24]

Pastor John Smyth left the Church of England in 1606 and joined the separatists who emigrated to Holland for refuge to escape the persecutions of James I. It was from this group that the Pilgrims left for the New World on the *Mayflower.* Smyth, who remained in Holland, became convinced that baptism was for converted professors of Christianity only. He and thirty-seven others were immersed, and "formed the first church composed of Englishmen that is known to have stood for the baptism of believers only."[25]

From this humble beginning the Baptist movement has spread over the world. Carey took it to India, Judson to Burma. It has become one of the strongest forces of Protestantism.

At the time of the Battle of Waterloo in 1815 there was no Baptist church on the continent of Europe,[26] yet today there are between two and three million Baptists there. They are strong in Romania. In Russia the Baptist Church developed vigorously. Its evangelistic labors began among the German settlers in southern Russia, following Oncken's motto, "Every member a missionary." First the Baptists labored among the German minority, and later among the Russians themselves. The Mennonites cooperated with the Baptists in certain places in an ecumenical spirit. The conversion in 1871 of Vasili Pavloff, who developed into a Russian evangelist, gave impetus to the growth of the work among the Russians. [27]

"Baptists have always regarded infant baptism not simply as an unauthorized and useless innovation, but as involving a radical departure from the purpose of Christ in instituting the ordinance: supplanting believers' baptism, making the symbol antedate the thing symbolized, striking at the root of regenerate church-membership, tending to bring the entire population of a Christianized community into church fellowship, and making possible and fostering State-churchism."[28]

## Other Christian Churches

In more recent times other Protestant and evangelical bodies have followed the Baptists in practice of baptism by immersion. One of the vigorous missionary movements during the past century is that of the Seventh-day Adventists, who sprang from the Millerite movement in the first half of the nineteenth century. William Miller was a Baptist lay preacher. Although ministers of many persuasions united with Miller in his second-advent preaching, the organization of the Seventh-day Adventist group was influenced greatly by James White, a minister of the Christian Church who believed in immersion. Apparently the denomination had no discussions regarding the adoption of immersion of responsible converts, as the mode of baptism. Though their membership is not large—1,500,000—they have become one of the most ubiquitous of religious bodies, carrying on mission work in almost every land on earth. Some of the largest baptisms have been held in the ancient strongholds of the Paulicians in Romania.[29]

### *Recent Revival of Adult Baptism in Anglican Communion*

Within the Anglican Church in recent years, there has been a growing spirit of protest against the baptizing of infants. Several vicars have resigned over the issue. Others have announced they will no longer baptize any but believing adults. Their position is encouraged by still others who have not yet taken an open stand.

As reported by *Time,* "The current rebellion against baptizing children has both practical and Scriptural motives. Many vicars are depressed by the number of non-churchgoing laymen who want to see their child christened merely as a matter of form. Other clergymen have also been convinced by their Scriptural studies that in apostolic times baptism was reserved for converted adults, and that Jesus' instruction—'Suffer little children . . . to come unto Me'—implies only a naming-and-blessing ceremony."[30]

Thus, though many innovations in the baptismal ceremony have been introduced since John baptized in the Jordan, the original New Testament rite, in its ancient form, has survived for almost twenty centuries. It is observed today by millions of Christians in many denominations around the world.

# References

## CHAPTER 1

1. Frederick Cornwallis Conybeare. "Baptism." *The Encyclopaedia Britannica,* 11th ed., Vol. 3, p. 364.

2. Tertullian, *On Baptism,* chap. 5. [Roberts, *Ante-Nicene Christian Library* (Edinburgh: T. & T. Clark, 1867-1872), Vol. 11, pp. 236, 237.]

3. Franz Cumont, *The Mysteries of Mithra* (Chicago: The Open Court Publishing Company, 1903), pp. 172, 173.

4. S. Krauss, "Baptism," *The Jewish Encyclopedia,* Vol. 2, p. 499.

5. Hugo Hahn, "Baptism," *The Universal Jewish Encyclopedia,* Vol. 2, p. 68.

6. Quoted in William Wall, *The History of Infant-Baptism* (Oxford: University Press, 1862), Vol. 1, pp. 4, 5.

7. *Ibid.,* p. 7.

8. Gemara, *tit. Jevamoth,* chap. 4, fol. 62:1. [Quoted in Wall, *Ibid.,* p. 19.]

9. Maimonides. [Quoted in J. A. Harding and T. L. Wilkinson, *Debate on Baptism: Embracing Mode and Subjects* (Toronto: William Briggs, 1886), p. 137.]

10. Gavin, *The Jewish Antecedents of the Christian Sacraments,* pp. 30-40, 55-58. [Quoted in Kenneth Scott Latourette, *A History of the Expansion of Christianity,* Vol. 1, *The First Five Centuries* (New York: Harper & Brothers, 1937), p. 304.]

11. Hans Lietzmann, *The Beginnings of the Christian Church* (New York: Charles Scribner's Sons, 1937), p. 80.

12. Adolph Harnack, *The Expansion of Christianity in the First Three Centuries* (London: Williams & Norgate, 1904), Vol. 1, p. 482.

## CHAPTER 2

1. Frederick Cornwallis Conybeare, "Baptism," *The Encyclopaedia Britannica,* 11th ed., Vol. 3, p. 369.

2. Kenneth Scott Latourette, *A History of the Expansion of Christianity,* Vol. 1, *The First Five Centuries* (New York: Harper & Brothers, 1937), pp. 116, 117.

3. ——, *A History of Christianity* (New York: Harper & Brothers, 1953), p. 76.

4. Edwin Hatch, *The Influence of Greek Ideas and Usages Upon the Christian Church* (London: Williams & Norgate, 1892), pp. 291-295.

5. Lyman Coleman, *The Antiquities of the Christian Church* (Andover: Gould, Newman & Saxton, 1841), p. 257.

6. *The Clementine Homilies,* Homily 9, chap. 19. [Roberts, *Ante-Nicene Christian Library* (Edinburgh: T. & T. Clark, 1867-1872), Vol. 17, p. 158.]

7. *The Didache,* chap. 7. [*The Apostolic Fathers,* translated by Glimm, Marique, and Walsh (New York: Cima Publishing Co., Inc., 1947), p. 177.]

8. Justin Martyr, *First Apology,* chap. 61. [*Ante-Nicene Christian Library,* Vol. 2, pp. 59, 60.]

9. "Baptism," *The New Schaff-Herzog Encyclopedia of Religious Knowledge,* Vol. 1, p. 437.

10. Tertullian, *De Corona,* chap. 3. [*Ante-Nicene Christian Library,* Vol. 11, p. 336.]

11. Basil, *De Spiritu Sanctu,* 27. [Quoted in Joseph Cullen Ayer, *A Source Book for Ancient Church History* (New York: Charles Scribner's Sons, 1913), p. 484.]

12. Tertullian, *On Baptism,* chap. 13. [*Ante-Nicene Christian Library,* Vol. 11, pp. 247, 248.]

13. Cyprian, *Epistle* 59:1. [*Ante-Nicene Christian Library,* Vol. 8, p. 251.]

14. *The Apostolical Constitutions,* Bk. 7:42. [*Ante-Nicene Christian Library,* Vol. 17, p. 203.]

15. Tertullian, *On Baptism,* chap. 4. [*Ante-Nicene Christian Library,* Vol. 11, p. 236.]

16. Cyril, *Joan,* 3:5. [Cited in Wolfred Nelson Cote, *The Archaeology of Baptism* (London: Yates and Alexander, 1876), p. 102.]

17. Cyprian, *Epistle* 75:12. [*Ante-Nicene Christian Library,* Vol. 8, p. 311.]

18. Frank Granger, *The Worship of the Romans* (London: Methuen & Co., 1895), p. 205.

19. Pope Leo, Sermon 14, *De Passiona.* [Cited in Cote, *The Archaeology of Baptism,* p. 102.]

20. Cornelius Clifford, "Athanasius," *The Catholic Encyclopedia,* Vol. 2, p. 36.

21. Tertullian, *On Baptism,* chap. 12. [*Ante-Nicene Christian Library,* Vol. 11, p. 45.]

22. Irenaeus. [Philip Schaff, *History of the Christian Church* (New York: Charles Scribner and Co., 1870), Vol. 1, p. 403.]

23. Cyprian, *Epistle* 73:7. [*Ante-Nicene Christian Library,* Vol. 8, p. 281.]

24. Schaff, *op. cit.,* Vol. 1, p. 401.

25. Robert Robinson, *The History of Baptism* (London: Thomas Knott, 1790), p. 282.

26. *The Didache,* chap. 7. [*The Apostolic Fathers,* p. 177.]

27. "Baptism," *The Encyclopaedia Britannica,* 11th ed., Vol. 3, pp. 364, 365.

28. Wolfred Nelson Cote, *The Archaeology of Baptism,* p. 80.

29. F. E. Warren, *The Liturgy and Ritual of the Ante-Nicene Church* (London: Society for Promoting Christian Knowledge, 1912), pp. 78, 79.

30. John Laurence von Mosheim, James Murdoch translator, *Institutes of Eccelesiastical History* (New York: Robert Carter and Brothers, 1832), Bk. 1, century 2, pt. 2, chap. 4, sec. 6.

31. Robinson, *op. cit.,* p. 511.

32. William Wall, *The History of Infant-Baptism* (Oxford: University Press, 1862), Vol. 2, p. 631.

33. Cyprian, *Epistle* 74. [*Ante-Nicene Christian Library,* Vol. 8, p. 293.]

34. "Baptism," *The Catholic Encyclopedia,* Vol. 2, p. 264.

35. *Ibid.,* pp. 264, 265.

36. Tertullian, *On Baptism,* chap. 16. [*Ante-Nicene Christian Library,* Vol. 11, p. 250.]

37. Fulgentius, *De Fide ad Petrum,* chap. 30. [Quoted in Wall, *op. cit.,* Vol. 1, p. 449.]

38. Cyprian, *Epistle* 53:4. [*Ante-Nicene Christian Library,* Vol. 8, p. 157.]

39. John Fulton, *Index Canonum* (New York: Pott, Young & Co., 1872), p. 217.

40. Cyprian, *Epistle* 75:12. [*Ante-Nicene Christian Library,* Vol. 8, pp. 311, 312.]

41. T. M. Lindsay, "Baptism," *International Standard Bible Encyclopedia,* Vol. 1, p. 390.

42. Basil, *Epistle 1, Ad Amphil.* [Cited in Baptism," *The Catholic Encyclopedia,* Vol. 2, p. 263.]

43. Jerome, *Contra Lucifer.* [Cited in *Ibid.*]

44. *Loc. cit.*

## CHAPTER 3

1. *The Didache,* chap. 7:1. [Glimm, *The Apostolic Fathers* (New York: Cima Publishing Co., Inc., 1947), p. 177.]

2. Tertullian, *Adversus Praxeam,* chap. 26. [Roberts, *Ante-Nicene Christian Library* (Edinburgh: T. & T. Clark, 1867-1872), Vol. 15, p. 395.]

3. ———, *De Corona, 3.* [*Ante-Nicene Christian Library,* Vol. 11, p. 336.]

4. Justin, *Apology* 1:61. [*Ante-Nicene Christian Library,* Vol. 2, p. 60.]

5. Hippolytus, *Canon 19,* par. 123-133. [F. E. Warren, *The Liturgy and Ritual of the Ante-Nicene Church* (London: 1912), p. 78.]

6. Ambrose, *De Sacramento,* Bk. 2, chap. 7. [Quoted in Bingham, *The Antiquities of the Christian Church,* Bk. 11, chap. 11, sec. 6 (London: Henry G. Bohn, 1852), Vol. 1, p. 539.]

7. J. H. Moore, "Trine Immersion," *The New Shaff-Herzog Encyclopedia of Religious Knowledge,* Vol. 12, p. 16.

8. Augustine, *Hom. 3, ap. Gratian de Consecrat,* Dist. 4, chap. 78. [Referred to in Bingham, *op. cit.,* Vol. 1, p. 540.]

9. Jerome, *Hieron. lib. 2 in Ephes.* 4, p. 122. [Quoted in Bingham, *loc. cit.*]

10. *The Apostolical Constitutions,* Bk. 8, canon 50. [*Ante-Nicene Christian Library,* Vol. 17, p. 263.]

11. Edward Mason, *The Gospel According to Jesus* (Dayton, Ohio: Press of the United Brethren Publishing House, 1888), p. 153.

12. J. F. Goggin, "African Liturgy," *The Catholic Encyclopedia,* Vol. 1, p. 196.

13. J. H. Moore, "Trine Immersion," *The New Schaff-Herzog Encylopedia of Religious Knowledge,* Vol. 12, p. 16.

14. William Wall, *The History of Infant-Baptism* (Oxford: University Press, 1862), Vol. 1, p. 592.

15. Wace and Schaff, *A Select Library of Nicene and Post-Nicene Fathers of the Christian Church,* Second Series (New York: The Christian Literature Company, 1890-1893), Vol. 6, p. 324.

16. Bingham, *op. cit.,* Bk. 11, chap. 11, sec. 7, Vol. 1, p. 540.

17. Michael Ott, "Martin of Braga," *The Catholic Encylopedia,* Vol. 9. p. 732.

18. John Henry Cardinal Newman, *Aryans of the Fourth Century.* 5th ed. (London: Longmans, Green, and Co., 1888), p. 89.

19. "Baptism," *The New Schaff-Herzog Encyclopedia of Religious Knowledge,* Vol. 1, p. 440.

20. Tertullian, *De Corona,* chap. 8, par. 3, 4. [*Ante-Nicene Christian Library,* Vol. 11, p. 337.]

21. *Ibid.,* p. 336.

22. Jerome, *The Dialogue Against the Luciferians,* par. 8. [*Nicene and Post-Nicene Fathers,* Vol. 6, p. 324.]

23. Basil, *De Spiritu Sancto,* 27. [Joseph Cullen Ayer, *A Source Book for Ancient History* (New York: Charles Scribner's Sons, 1913), pp. 484, 485.]

24. Theodoret, *Haeret, Fabul.,* Bk. 4, chap. 3. [Cited in Bingham, *op. cit.,* Vol. 1, p. 623.]

25. *The Ecclesiastical History of Sozomen,* Bk. 6, chap. 26. [*Nicene and Post-Nicene Fathers,* Vol. 2, p. 363.]

26. Gregory, *Epistle to Leandro.* [Cited in Wall, *op. cit.,* Vol. 1, p. 594.]

27. *Collección de Cánones de la Iglesia Española* (Madrid: D. Anselmo Santa Coloma y Companía, 1850), Vol. 2, pp. 267, 268, Canon 6. (Translated by H. F. Brown.)

28. Frederick Cornwallis Conybeare, "Baptism," *The Encyclopaedia Britannica,* 11th ed., Vol. 3, p. 366.

29. *Ibid.*

30. F. Kattenbusch, "Baptism," *The New Schaff-Herzog Encyclopedia of Religious Knowledge,* Vol. 1, p. 437.

## CHAPTER 4

1. Eduardo Cierra y Prat, *Razón de la Liturgia Católica* (Barcelona: Libería Católica Internacional, 1929), p. 323.

2. Alexander V. G. Allen, *Christian Institutions* (New York: Charles Scribner's Sons, 1906), pp. 406, 407.

3. William Wall, *The History of Infant-Baptism* (Oxford: University Press, 1862), Vol. 1, p. 17.

4. Justin Martyr, *Apology* 1, chap. 15. [Roberts, *Ante-Nicene Christian Library* (Edinburgh: T. & T. Clark, 1867-1872), Vol. 2, p. 18.]

5. Irenaeus, *Against Heresies,* Bk. 2, chap. 22:4. [*Ante-Nicene Christian Library,* Vol. 5, p. 200.]

6. Wall, *op. cit.,* p. 49.

7. Tertullian, *On Baptism,* chap. 18. [*Ante-Nicene Christian Library,* Vol. 11, p. 253.]

8. *Ibid.,* p. 254.

9. Augustus Neander, *The History of the Christian Religion and the Church,* Rose translation (New York: Stanford and Swords, 1848), p. 199.

10. James F. Loughlin, "Ambrose," *The Catholic Encyclopedia,* Vol. 1, p. 384.

11. Frederick Cornwallis Conybeare, "Baptism," *The Encyclopaedia Britannica,* 11th ed., Vol. 3, p. 366.

12. D. O. Hunter-Blair, "Gregory of Nazianzus," *The Catholic Encyclopedia,* Vol. 7, p. 11.

13. Richard Travers Smith, *St. Basil the Great* (London: Society for Promoting Christian Knowledge, 1879), p. 20.

14. Wall, *op. cit.,* pp. 38 5, 392.

15. *Ibid.,* 389.

16. *Ibid.,* pp. 636 ff.

17. Louis Saltet, "Jerome," *The Catholic Encyclopedia,* Vol. 8, p. 341.

18. Conybeare, *loc. cit.*

19. Wall, *op. cit.,* p. 212.

20. *The Constitutions of the Apostles,* Bk. 6, chap. 15. [*Ante-Nicene Christian Library,* Vol. 17, p. 159.]

21. Origen, *Homily 8 in Lev.,* chap. 4. [Quoted in Wall, *op. cit.,* p. 65.]

22. ——, *Homily in Lucam* 14. [Quoted in Wall, *loc. cit.*]

23. ——, *Com. in Epist. ad Romanos,* Bk. 5, chap. 9. [Quoted in Wall, *op. cit.,* p. 66.]

24. Adolph Harnack. [Quoted in A. R. Main, *Baptism: Our Lord's Command* (Melbourne: Australia Publishing Co., 1913), p. 125.]

25. Cyprian, *Ep. 58, "To Fidus,"* par. 2. [*Ante-Nicene Christian Library,* Vol. 8, pp. 196, 197.]

26. Charles Joseph Hefele, *History of the Councils of the Church* (Edinburgh: T. & T. Clark, 1876), Vol. 2, p. 458.

27. Augustine, *De Genesi ad Literam,* Bk. 10, par. 39. [Quoted in Wall, *op. cit.,* Vol. 1, p. 179.]

28. Augustine, *De Baptismo contra Donatistas.* [Quoted in Wall, *op. cit.,* Vol. 1, p. 159.]

29. Basil, *Oratio Exhortatoria ad Baptismum,* sec. 1. [Quoted in Wall, *op. cit.,* Vol. 1, p. 131.]

30. Gregory Nazianzus, *Oratio de Baptismo,* Or. 40, par. 7. [Quoted in Wall, *op. cit.,* Vol. 1, p. 111.]

31. Charles W. Bennett, *Christian Archeology* (*Library of Biblical and Theological Literature,* Vol. 4, Crooks and Hurst, editors. New York: Hunt and Eaton, 1891), p. 393.

32. Philip Schaff, *History of the Christian Church* (New York: Charles Scribner and Co., 1870-1891), Vol. 1, p. 402.

33. *Ibid.,* Vol. 2, p. 255.

34. John Henry Cardinal Newman, *Development of Christian Doctrine* (London: Longmans, Green, and Co., 1897), p. 129.

35. Robert Robinson, *The History of Baptism* (London: Thomas Knott, 1790), p. 269.

36. T. B. Scannell, "Confirmation," *The Catholic Encyclopedia,* Vol. 4, p. 216.

37. Gregory Nazianzus, *Orat.* 40:23. [Quoted by P. J. Toner in "Limbo," *The Catholic Encyclopedia,* Vol. 9, p. 256.]

38. *Ibid.,* p. 257.

39. Cyprian, *On the Lapsed,* par. 25. [*Ante-Nicene Christian Library,* Vol. 8, pp. 368, 369.]

40. *Dogmatic Canons and Decrees* (New York: The Devin-Adair Company, 1912), Council of Trent, Ses. 21, Canon 4, p. 130.

41. *Canons of Hippolytus,* Canon 19, par. 113. [Cited in F. E. Warren, *The Liturgy and Ritual of the Ante-Nicene Church* (London: Society for Promoting Christian Knowledge, 1912), p. 58.]

42. Tertullian, *On Baptism,* chap. 18. [*Ante-Nicene Christian Library,* Vol. 11, p. 253.]

43. Bertrand L. Conway, *The Question-Box Answers* (New York: The Paulist Press, 1925), p. 259.

CHAPTER 5

1. *Colección de Cánones de la Iglesia Española* (Madrid: D. Anselmo Santa Coloma y Companía, 1849), Vol. 1, p. 48. (Translated by H. F. Brown.)

2. *The Didache,* chap. 7. [Glimm, *The Apostolic Fathers* (New York: Cima Publishing Co., Inc., 1947, p. 177.]

3. Gregory of Nyssa, *The Great Catechism,* chap. 35. [Wace and Schaff, *A Select Library of Nicene and Post-Nicene Fathers of the Christian Church,* Second Series (New York: The Christian Literature Company, 1890-1893), Vol. 5, p. 503.]

4. E. de Pressensé, *Christian Life and Practice in the Early Church* (London: Hodder and Stoughton, 1877), p. 36.

5. Cyprian, *Epistle,* 75:12. [Roberts, *Ante-Nicene Christian Library* (Edinburgh: T. & T. Clark, 1867-1872), Vol. 8, pp. 311, 312.]

6. James Cardinal Gibbons, *The Faith of Our Fathers,* Holy Name Edition (New York: The Holy Name Society, 1929), pp. 277, 278.

7. Pamelius. [Quoted in B. F. Snook, *The Nature, Subjects and Design of Christian Baptism* (Battle Creek, Mich.: Steam Press of the Review and Herald Office, 1861), pp. 42, 43.]

8. William Wall, *The History of Infant-Baptism* (Oxford: University Press, 1862), Vol. 1, p. 576.

9. Robert Robinson, *The History of Baptism* (London: Thomas Knott, 1790), p. 113.

10. "Baptism," *The Edinburgh Encyclopedia.* [Quoted in Snook, *op. cit.,* p. 44.]

11. Sozomen, *Lib.* 6, chap. 6. [*A Select Library of Nicene and Post-Nicene Fathers of the Christian Church,* Second Series, Vol. 2, p. 350.]

12. Robinson, *op. cit.* p. 132.

13. *Ibid.,* p. 417.

14. Tertullian, *On Baptism,* chap. 5. [*Ante-Nicene Christian Library,* Vol. 11, p. 236.]

15. S. Baring-Gould, *The Origin and Development of Religious Belief* (London: Longmans, Green, and Co., 1892), Vol. 1, p. 397.

16. Franz Cumont, *The Mysteries of Mithra* (Chicago: Open Court Publishing Company, 1903), p. 157.

17. Virgil, *Aeneid,* 6. [Quoted in Wolfred Nelson Cote, *The Archaeology of Baptism* (London: Yates and Alexander, 1876), p. 3.]

18. *Ibid.,* 2. [Quoted in Robinson, *op. cit.,* p. 41.]

19. Pliny, *Nat. Hist.,* 5:30. [Cited in Robinson, *loc. cit.*]

20. Ovid, *Fast.* 4:2. [Cited in Robinson, *loc. cit.*]

21. Samuel Angus, *The Mystery-Religions and Christianity* (New York: Charles Scribner's Sons, 1925), p. 82.

22. Frank Granger, *The Worship of the Romans* (London: Methuen & Co., 1895), p. 204.

23. Franz Cumont, *After Life in Roman Paganism* (New Haven, Conn.: Yale University Press, 1922), p. 118.

24. *Catechism According to the Decree of the Council of Trent,* English translation by the Very Rev. J. Donovan (Dublin: James Duffy and Company, 1829), pp. 149, 150.

25. *Ibid.*

26. *A Catechism of Christian Doctrine,* No. 3, Revised Edition of the Baltimore Catechism (Patterson, N.J.: St. Anthony Guild Press, 1949), p. 260.

## CHAPTER 6

1. Wolfred Nelson Cote, *The Archaeology of Baptism* (London: Yates and Alexander, 1876), p. 16.

2. Pastor of Hermas, *Simil.* 9, chap. 16. [Roberts, *Ante-Nicene Christian Library* (Edinburgh: T. & T. Clark, 1867-1872), Vol. 1, p. 420.]

3. Justin Martyr, *First Apology,* chap. 61. [*Ante-Nicene Christian Library,* Vol. 2, p. 59.]

4. Tertullian, *Adversus Praxean,* chap. 26. [*Ante-Nicene Christian Library,* Vol. 15, p. 395.]

5. Hippolytus, *Discourse on the Holy Theophany,* sec. 10. [*Ante-Nicene Christian Library,* Vol. 9, part 2, p. 87.]

6. Porphyry, *Macarius Magnes,* 4:19. [Quoted in Adolph Harnack, *The Expansion of Christianity in the First Three Centuries* (London: Williams & Norgate, 1904), Vol. 1, p. 484.]

7. Cyril of Jerusalem, *Catech.* 3, 17. [Quoted in Cote, *op. cit.,* p. 22.]

8. Basil, *Homil.* 13, "Exhor. Ad Bapt." [Quoted in Robert Robinson, *The History of Baptism* (London: Thomas Knott, 1790), p. 66.]

9. Ambrose, *De Sacram.,* Bk. 2, chap. 7. [Quoted in Bingham, *The Antiquities of the Christian Church* (London: Henry G. Bohn, 1852), Bk. 11, chap. 11, sec. 4.]

10. Henry Jenner, "Ambrosian Liturgy and Rite," *The Catholic Encyclopedia,* Vol. 1, p. 403.

11. Augustine, *Hom. 4.* [Quoted in Isaac Taylor Hinton, *A History of Baptism* (Philadelphia: American Baptist Publication and S.S. Society, 1840), p. 164.]

12. Zeno, *Invitat. 2 ad Bapt. Bibl. Max. Patr.,* Vol. 2, p. 442. [Quoted in Cote, *op. cit.,* p. 196.]

13. Gregory of Nyssa, *On the Baptism of Christ.* [Quoted in Wace, *A Select Library of Nicene and Post-Nicene Fathers of the Christian Church,* Second Series (New York: The Christian Literature Company, 1890-1893), Vol. 5. p. 520.]

14. Clovis, *Letter to the Canons of Lyons.* [Quoted in William Cathcart, *The Baptism of the Ages and of the Nations* (Philadelphia: American Baptist Publication Society, 1878), p. 89.]

15. *Ibid.,* p. 87.

16. *Const. Eccles. Egypt.* 2:46. [Cited in E. de Pressensé, *Christian Life and Practice in the Early Church* (London: Hodder and Stoughton, 1877), p. 34.]

17. Council of Celchyth, *Canon 6.* [Quoted in Cote, *op. cit.,* pp. 234, 235.]

18. *Ibid.,* p. 284.

19. Bonaventure, *librum 4. Sententiarum, Distinct.* 3, Art. 2. Quaest. 2. [Quoted in William Wall, *The History of Infant-Baptism* (Oxford: University Press, 1862), Vol. 1, p. 575.]

20. Thomas Aquinas, *Summa Theologiae,* Part 3, Quaest. 66, Art. 7. [Quoted in Wall, *loc. cit.*]

21. Michael J. O'Farrell, *Popular Life of St. Patrick* (New York, 1863), p. 110.

22. *De Rel. Eccl.* c. 216. [Quoted in Philip Schaff, *History of the Christian Church* (New York: Charles Scribner's Sons, 1891), Vol. 2, p. 250.]

23. Cote, *op. cit.,* p. 254.

24. John Calvin, *Institutes of the Christian Religion,* translated by John Allen (London: Thomas Tegg, 1844), Bk. 4, chap. 15, sec. 19, Vol. 2, p. 434.

25. "Baptism," *The Edinburgh Encyclopedia.* [Cited by L. C. Wilson, *The History of Sprinkling* (Cincinnati, Ohio: Standard Publishing Company, 1895), p. 10.]

26. "Baptism," *The Edinburgh Encyclopedia.* [Quoted by Hinton, *A History of Baptism,* p. 195.]

27. *Luther's Works,* ed. of 1551, Vol. 2, p. 76. [Quoted by Cote, *op. cit.,* p. 261.]

28. Martin Luther, *De Sacram. Bapt.* op. Tom. 1, fol. 72. [Cited in T. J. Conant, *The Meaning and Use of Baptism* (New York: American Bible Union, 1864), pp. 160, 161.]

29. Luther, *Werke,* Irmischeid ed., Vol. 21, p. 229. [Cited in Conant, *op. cit.,* p. 146. Translated by H. F. Brown.]

30. Schaff, *op. cit.,* Vol. 2, p. 251, footnote.

31. August Neander, *Lectures on the History of Christian Dogmas* (London: Henry G. Bohn, 1858), Vol. 2, p. 692.

32. *Proceedings of the Assembly of Divines From Jan. 1, 1643, to Dec. 31, 1644* (London, 1824), Vol. 13, pp. 300, 301.

33. *Ibid.*

34. J. H. Blunt, *Dictionary of Sects, Heresies, Ecclesiastical Parties, and Schools of Religious Thought* (London: Rivingtons, 1874), p. 320.

35. Moore, *Life of Wesley*, Vol. 1, p. 425. [Cited in Edward Mason, *The Gospel According to Jesus* (Dayton, Ohio: Press of the United Brethren Publishing House, 1888), p. 160.]

36. G. Elsie Harrison, *Son to Susanna* (Nashville: Cokesbury Press, 1938), pp. 135, 161.

37. *The Journal of the Rev. John Wesley,* Everyman's Edition (London: J. M. Dent and Sons, 1913), Vol. 1, pp. 24, 29.

38. John Wesley, *Explanatory Notes Upon the New Testament* (London: John Mason, 1831), Vol. 2, p. 28.

39. John Telford, *Life of John Wesley* (New York: Phillips and Hunt, 1887), p. 303.

40. Arthur Penrhyn Stanley, *Christian Institutions* (New York: Charles Scribner's Sons, 1881), p. 21.

41. Lyman Coleman, *Ancient Christianity Exemplified* (Philadelphia: Lippincott, 1875), pp. 396, 397.

## CHAPTER 7

1. Justin Martyr, *Apology* 1, chap. 61. [Roberts, *Ante-Nicene Christian Library* (Edinburgh: T. & T. Clark, 1867-1872), Vol. 2, p. 59.]

2. Clement, *Homily* 9, chap. 19. [*Ante-Nicene Christian Library,* Vol. 17, p. 158.]

3. John Alfred Faulkner, *Cyprian: The Churchman* (Cincinnati: Jennings and Graham, 1906), p. 25.

4. Tertullian, *On Baptism,* chap. 4. [*Ante-Nicene Christian Library,* Vol. 11, p. 235.]

5. Walter Lowrie, *Monuments of the Early Church* (New York: The Macmillan Company, 1901), pp. 135, 136.

6. John B. Peterson, "Baptismal Font," *The Catholic Encyclopedia,* Vol. 2, p. 274.

7. *Colección de Cánones de la Iglesia de Española* (Madrid: D. Anselmo Santa Colma y Companía, 1850), Vol. 2, pp. 597, 598. (Translated by H. F. Brown.)

8. Baronius, *Annales,* Ann. 384. [Cited in Robert Robinson, *The History of Baptism* (London: Thomas Knott, 1790), p. 60.]

9. Thomas H. Poole, "Baptistery," *The Catholic Encyclopedia,* Vol. 2, p. 277.

10. John B. Peterson, *op. cit.,* p. 275.

11. Hatchett's *Guide,* p. 313.

12. *Ibid.,* p. 337.

13. *Ibid.,* p. 396.

14. *Ibid.,* p. 426.

15. *Ibid.,* p. 226.

16. *Ibid.,* p. 59.

17. H. V. Morton, *Through Lands of the Bible* (New York: Dodd, Mead & Company, 1938), p. 132.

18. Jack Finegan, *Light From the Ancient Past* (Princeton University Press, 1946), p. 454.

19. *Ibid.,* p. 447.

20. Wolfred Nelson Cote, *The Archaeology of Baptism* (London: Yates and Alexander, 1876), pp. 325, 326.

21. Robert Robinson, *The History of Baptism* (London: Thomas Knott, 1790), p. 63.

22. Michael Lopez, *Battistero di Parma,* p. 120. [Quoted in Cote, *op. cit.,* p. 206.]

23. U. Benigui, "Verona," *The Catholic Encyclopedia,* Vol. 15, p. 360.

24. Charles W. Bennett, *Christian Archeology* (*Library of Biblical and Theological Literature,* Vol. 4, Crooks and Hurst, editors. New York: Hunt and Eaton, 1891), p. 412.

25. Cote, *op. cit.,* pp. 175, 176.

26. Racca, *Dei Duomo e del Battistero di Novara.* [Cited in Cote, *op. cit.,* p. 190.]

27. *Ibid.,* p. 207.

28. Cardinal Bullion, *Historia Templi Vaticani,* chap. 22. [Quoted in Cote, *op. cit.,* p. 208.]

29. Valentini, *Basilica Vaticana,* Vol. 2. [Quoted in Cote, *op. cit.,* p. 209.]

30. *Ibid.*

31. Cote, *op. cit.,* p. 185.

32. Thomas H. Poole, "Baptistery," *The Catholic Encyclopedia,* Vol. 2, p. 277.

33. Cote, *op. cit.,* p. 257.

34. *Ibid.,* pp. 257, 258.

35. *Ibid.,* p. 259.

36. Abbé Fleury, *Histoire Ecclésiastique.* [Quoted in Cote, *op. cit.,* p. 259.]

37. Robinson, *op. cit.,* p. 113.

38. William Cathcart, *The Baptism of the Ages and of the Nations* (Philadelphia: American Baptist Publication Society, 1878), p. 91.

39. Cote, *op. cit.,* pp. 255, 256.

40. F. Simpson, Jun., *A Series of Ancient Baptismal Fonts Chronologically Arranged* (London: Septimus Prowett, 1828), preface, p. vii.

41. *Ibid.,* preface, pp. xiv, xv.

42. *Ibid.,* p. 23.

43. *Ibid.,* p. 36.

44. *Ibid.,* p. 46.

45. *Ibid.,* p. 48.

46. *Ibid.,* p. 56.

47. *Constitutiones Edmundi,* Canon 10. [Quoted in Cote, *op. cit.,* p. 243.]

48. Robinson, *op. cit.,* p. 124.

49. *The Catholic Encyclopedia,* Vol. 2, p. 277.

50. R. Brown, *Sacred Architecture.* [Quoted in Cote, *op. cit.,* p. 243.]

51. Cote, *op. cit.,* pp. 244, 245.

52. Cathcart, *op. cit.,* pp. 59, 60.

53. Simpson, *op. cit.,* preface, p. xvi.

## CHAPTER 8

1. Philip Schaff, *Teaching of the Twelve Apostles,* pp. 36-41. [Quoted in Camden M. Cobern, *The New Archeological Discoveries,* 6th ed. (New York: Funk and Wagnalls Company, 1921), p. 400.]

2. William Ingraham Kip, *The Catacombs of Rome* (New York: Redfield, 1854), p. 118.

3. Bertoli, *Antichitá d' Aquileja.* [Quoted in Wolfred Nelson Cote, *The Archaeology of Baptism* (London: Yates and Alexander, 1876), p. 189.]

4. Cote, *The Archaeology of Baptism,* p. 195.

5. Martini, *Theatrum Basilicae Pisanae,* Appendix. [Cited in Cote, *op. cit.,* p. 203.]

6. Cote, *op. cit.,* p. 260.

7. *Ibid.,* pp. 220, 221.

8. *Ibid.,* p. 222.

9. John B. Peterson, "Baptismal Font," *The Catholic Encyclopedia,* Vol. 2, p. 274.

10. Cote, *op. cit.,* pp. 42, 43.

11. *Ibid.,* pp. 45, 46.

12. *Ibid.,* pp. 40, 41.


## CHAPTER 9

1. Moses Gaster, "Bogomils," *The Encyclopaedia Britannica,* 11th ed., Vol. 4, p. 119.

2. Gilbert Burnet, *History of the Reformation* (Oxford: University Press, 1829), Vol. 1, preface, p. xii.

3. Moore, *Life of Wesley* (New York, 1825), Vol. 2, p. 127.

4. Jesse Forest Silver, *The Lord's Return* (New York: Fleming H. Revell Company, 1914), p. 72.

5. John T. Christian, *A History of the Baptists* (Nashville: Broadman Press, 1922), p. 43.

6. John Laurence von Mosheim, James Murdock, translator, *Institutes of Ecclesiastical History* (New York: Robert Carter and Brothers, 1832), Bk. 1, century 3, pt. 2, chap. 5, sec. 18.

7. Albert Henry Newman, *A History of Anti-Pedobaptism* (Philadelphia: American Baptist Publication Society, 1896), p. 19.

8. Silver, *op. cit.,* p. 89.

9. Arthur Penrhyn Stanley, *Lectures on the History of the Eastern Church* (London: John Murray, 1864), p. 296.

10. K. R. Hagenbach, *A Text-Book of the History of Doctrines* (New York: Sheldon and Company, 1867), Vol. 2, p. 85.

11. Paul Daniel Alphandéry, "Albigenses," *The Encyclopaedia Britannica,* 11th ed., Vol. 1, p. 505.

12. Christian, *op. cit.,* p. 60.

13. *Ibid.,* p. 61.

14. Emil Comba, *History of the Waldenses* (London, 1889), p. 17. [Cited in Christian, *op. cit.,* p. 64.]

15. Newman, *op. cit.,* p. 30.

16. Christian, *op. cit.,* p. 65.

17. *Ibid.,* p. 87.

18. *Ibid.,* p. 94.

19. L'Abbe Fleury, *Historae Eccles.,* 34:282. [Quoted in Christian, *op. cit.,* p. 115.]

20. Christian, *op. cit.,* p. 95.

21. Mosheim, *op. cit.,* Bk. 4, century 16, sec. 3, pt. 2, chap. 3, sec. 2.

22. Henry C. Vedder, *Short History of the Baptists* (Philadelphia and New York: The American Baptist Publication Society, 1907), p. 185.

23. *Ibid.,* p. 187.

24. *Ibid.,* p. 201.

25. *Ibid.,* p. 203.

26. J. H. Rushbrooke, *The Baptist Movement in the Continent of Europe* (London: Kingsgate Press, 1923), p. 5.

27. *Ibid.,* p. 134.

28. Newman, *op. cit.,* pp. 28, 29.

29. From personal observation by the author.

30. *Time,* Jan. 8, 1965, p. 36.

# Bibliography

Allen, Alexander V. G. *Christian Institutions.* New York: Charles Scribner's Sons, 1906. 577 pages.

Andrews, J. N. and L. R. Conradi. *History of the Sabbath,* 4th ed., rev. Washington, D.C.: Review and Herald Publishing Association, 1912. 864 pages.

Angus, Samuel. *The Mystery-Religions and Christianity.* New York: Charles Scribner's Sons, 1925. 359 pages.

Ayer, Joseph Cullen. *A Source Book for Ancient Church History From the Apostolic Age to the Close of the Conciliar Period.* New York: Charles Scribner's Sons, 1913. 707 pages.

Baring-Gould, S. *The Origin and Development of Religious Belief,* part 1, new ed. London: Longmans, Green, and Co., 1892. 422 pages.

Bennett, Charles W. *Christian Archeology.* Vol. 4 of *Library of Biblical and Theological Literature,* edited by George R. Crooks and John F. Hurst. New York: Hunt and Eaton, 1891. 558 pages.

Bingham, Joseph. *The Antiquities of the Christian Church,* Vol. 1. London: Henry G. Bohn, 1852. 676 pages.

Blunt, J. H., ed. *Dictionary of Sects, Heresies, Ecclesiastical Parties, and Schools of Religious Thought.* London: Rivingtons, 1874. 647 pages.

Burnet, Gilbert. *History of the Reformation*, Vol. 1. Oxford: University Press, 1829.

Calvin, John. *Institutes of the Christian Religion*, translated by John Allen, Vol. 2. London: Thomas Tegg, 1844.

Cathcart, William. *The Baptism of the Ages and of the Nations*. Philadelphia: American Baptist Publication Society, 1878. 222 pages.

Christian, John T. *A History of the Baptists*. Nashville, Tennessee: Broadman Press, 1922. 408 pages.

Chrystal, James. *A History of the Modes of Christian Baptism*. Philadelphia: Lindsay and Blakiston, 1861. 324 pages.

Cirera y Prat, Eduardo. *Razón de la Liturgia Católica*. Barcelona: Librería Católica Internacional, 1929.

Cobern, Camden M. *The New Archeological Discoveries*, 6th ed. New York: Funk and Wagnalls Company, 1921. 708 pages.

*Colección de Cánones de la Iglesia Española,* published in Latin by Don Francisco Antonio Gonzales, translated into Spanish with notes and illustrations by Don Juan Tejada y Ramiro. Madrid: D. Anselmo Santa Coloma y Companía, 1849. 5 vols.

Coleman, Lyman. *Ancient Christianity Exemplified in the Private, Domestic, Social, and Civil Life of the Primitive Christians and in the Original Institutions, Offices, Ordinances, and Rites of the Church.* Philadelphia: J. B. Lippincott and Company, 1875. 645 pages.

——. *The Antiquities of the Christian Church.* Andover: Gould, Newman & Saxton, 1841. (Boston: Tappan and Dennett.) 557 pages.

Conant, T. J. *The Meaning and Use of Baptizm.* New York: American Bible Union, 1868. 163 pages.

Conway, Bertrand L. *The Question-Box Answers.* New York: The Paulist Press, 1925. 410 pages.

Cote, Wolfred Nelson. *The Archaeology of Baptism.* London: Yates and Alexander, 1876. 336 pages.

Cumont, Franz. *The Mysteries of Mithra,* translated from the second revised French edition by Thomas J. McCormack. Chicago: The Open Court Publishing Company, 1903. 239 pages.

——. *After Life in Roman Paganism.* New Haven: Yale University Press, 1922. 225 pages.

De Pressensé, E. *Christian Life and Practice in the Early Church,* translated by Annie Harwood-Holmden. London: Hodder and Stoughton, 1877. 528 pages.

*Dogmatic Canons and Decrees.* New York: The Devin-Adair Company, 1912. 257 pages.

Donovan, J., trans. *Catechism According to the Decrees of the Council of Trent.* Dublin: James Duffy and Company, Ltd., 1829. 534 pages.

Faulkner, John Alfred. *Cyprian: The Churchman.* Cincinnati: Jennings and Graham, 1906. 226 pages.

Finegan, Jack. *Light From the Ancient Past.* Princeton University Press, 1946. **500 pages.**

Firey, M. J. *Infant Salvation*. New York and London: Funk and Wagnalls Company, 1901. 407 pages.

Frazer, James George. *The Golden Bough, a Study in Magic and Religion*. New York: The Macmillan Company, 1922. 752 pages.

Fulton, John. *Index Canonum*. New York: Pott, Young & Co., 1872. 393 pages.

Gardner, Alice. *History of Sacrament in Relation to Thought and Progress*. London: Williams and Norgate, 1921. 189 pages.

Gibbons, James Cardinal. *The Faith of Our Fathers*. Holy Name Edition. New York: The Holy Name Society, 1929. 430 pages.

Glimm, Francis S., Joseph M.-F. Marique, and Gerald G. Walsh, *The Apostolic Fathers*. New York: Cima Publishing Company, Inc., 1947. 401 pages.

Granger, Frank. *The Worship of the Romans, Viewed in Relation to the Roman Temperament*. London: Methuen and Company, 1895. 313 pages.

Hagenbach, K. R. *A Text-Book of the History of Doctrines*, Vol. 2. New York: Sheldon and Company, 1867.

Harding, J. A., and T. L. Wilkinson. *Debate on Baptism: Embracing Mode and Subjects*. Toronto: William Briggs, 1886. 406 pages.

Harnack, Adolf. *The Expansion of Christianity in the First Three Centuries*, translated and edited by James Moffatt, Vol. 1. London: Williams & Norgate, 1904. 494 pages.

Harrison, G. Elsie, *Son to Susanna*. Nashville: Cokesbury Press, 1938.

Hatch, Edwin. *The Influence of Greek Ideas and Usages Upon the Christian Church*, 4th ed., edited by A. M. Fairbairn. London: Williams & Norgate, 1892. 359 pages.

Hefele, Charles Joseph. *A History of the Councils of the Church, From the Original Documents*, translated from the German by Henry Nutcombe Oxenham, Vol. 2. Edinburgh: T. & T. Clark, 1876. 503 pages.

Heron, James. *The Church of the Sub-Apostolic Age*. London: Hodder and Stoughton, 1888. 300 pages.

Hinton, Isaac Taylor. *A History of Baptism, Both From the Inspired and Uninspired Writings*. Philadelphia: American Baptist Publication and S.S. Society, 1840. 372 pages.

Kip, William Ingraham. *The Catacombs of Rome*. New York: Redfield, 1854. 212 pages.

——. *The Church of the Apostles*. New York: D. Appleton and Company, 1877. 174 pages.

Latourette, Kenneth Scott. *A History of Christianity*. New York: Harper and Brothers Publishers, 1953. 1,516 pages.

——. *The First Five Centuries*. Vol. 1 of *A History of the Expansion of Christianity*. New York and London: Harper and Brothers Publishers, 1937. 412 pages.

Lietzmann, Hans. *The Beginnings of the Christian Church*, translated by Bertram Lee Woolf. New York: Charles Scribner's Sons, 1937. 406 pages.

Lowrie, Walter. *Monuments of the Early Church*. New York: The Macmillan Company, 1901. 432 pages.

Main, A. R. *Baptism: Our Lord's Command.* Melbourne: Australia Publishing Company, 1913.

Mason, Edward. *The Gospel According to Jesus.* Dayton, Ohio: Press of the United Brethren Publishing House, 1888. 315 pages.

Mead, Frank S. *Handbook of Denominations.* Nashville: Abingdon-Cokesbury Press, 1951. 207 pages.

Moore, *Life of Wesley,* Vol. 2, New York, 1825.

Morton, H. V. *In the Steps of St. Paul.* London: Rich and Cowan, Ltd., 1936. 440 pages.

——. *Through Lands of the Bible.* New York: Dodd, Mead & Company, 1938. 452 pages.

Mosheim, John Laurence von, translated by James Murdock. *Institutes of Ecclesiastical History.* New York: Robert Carter and Brothers, 1832.

Neander, Augustus. *Lectures on the History of Christian Dogmas,* translated by J. E. Byland, Vol. 2, London: Henry G. Bohn, 1858.

——. *Memorials of Christian Life in the Early and Middle Ages,* translated from the German by J. E. Ryland. London: Henry G. Bohn, 1852. 538 pages.

——. *The History of the Christian Religion and the Church, During the Three First Centuries,* translated from the German by Henry John Rose, 2d ed. New York: Stanford and Swords, 1848. 466 pages.

Newman, Albert Henry. *A History of Anti-Pedobaptism; From the Rise of Pedobaptism to A.D. 1609.* Philadelphia: American Baptist Publication Society, 1896. 414 pages.

Newman, John Henry Cardinal. *An Essay on the Development of Christian Doctrine,* 10th ed. London: Longmans, Green, and Co., 1897. 445 pages.

——. *The Aryans of the Fourth Century,* 5th ed. London: Longmans, Green, and Co., 1888. 474 pages.

Nichol, Francis D. *The Midnight Cry; a Defense of William Miller and the Millerites.* Washington, D.C.: Review and Herald Publishing Association, 1944. 560 pages.

O'Brien, John A. *The Faith of Millions.* Bishop of Fort Wayne, Indiana. Huntington, Indiana: Our Sunday Visitor, 1938, 538 pages.

O'Farrell, Michael J. *Popular Life of St. Patrick.* New York, 1863.

*Proceedings of the Assembly of Divines, From Jan. 1, 1643, to Dec. 31, 1644,* Vol. 13. London, 1824.

Roberts, Alexander, and James Donaldson, eds. *Ante-Nicene Christian Library.* Edinburgh: T. & T. Clark, 1867-72. 24 vols.

Robinson, Robert. *The History of Baptism.* London: Thomas Knott, 1790. 653 pages.

Rushbrooke, J. H. *The Baptist Movement in the Continent of Europe.* London: Kingsgate Press, 1923. 207 pages.

Schaff, David S. *Our Fathers' Faith and Ours.* New York: G. P. Putnam's Sons, 1928. 680 pages.

Schaff, Philip. *History of the Christian Church,* Vols. 1, 2, 6. New York: Charles Scribner and Co., 1870-1891.

Silver, Jesse Forest. *The Lord's Return.* New York: Fleming H. Revell Company, 1914. 311 pages.

Simpson, F., Jun. *A Series of Ancient Baptismal Fonts, Chronologically Arranged.* London: Septimus Prowett, 1828.

Smith, Richard Travers. *St. Basil the Great.* London: Society for Promoting Christian Knowledge, 1879.

Snook, B. F. *The Nature, Subjects and Design of Christian Baptism.* Battle Creek, Michigan: Steam Press of the Review and Herald Office, 1861. 91 pages.

Stanley, Arthur Penrhyn. *Christian Institutions.* New York: Charles Scribner's Sons, 1881. 396 pages.

——. *Lectures on the History of the Eastern Church,* 3d ed. London: John Murray, 1864. 437 pages. (New York: Charles Scribner's Sons, 1900. 422 pages.)

Sullivan, John F. *The Visible Church.* New York: P. J. Kenedy and Sons, 1922. 278 pages.

Telford, John. *Life of John Wesley.* New York: Phillips and Hunt, 1887. 363 pages.

Tyler, J. Endell. *Primitive Christian Worship: or, the Evidence of Holy Scripture and the Church, Against the Invocation of Saints and Angels and the Blessed Virgin Mary,* Vol. 1. London: Society for Promoting Christian Knowledge, 1846. 415 pages.

Vedder, Henry C. *A Short History of the Baptists,* new and illustrated edition. Philadelphia: American Baptist Publication Society, 1907. 431 pages.

Wace, Henry, and Philip Schaff, eds. *A Select Library of Nicene and Post-Nicene Fathers of the Christian Church.* Second Series. Oxford: James Parker and Company; New York: The Christian Literature Company, 1890-1893. 6 vols.

Wall, William. *The History of Infant-Baptism, Together with Mr. Cale's Reflections, and Dr. Wall's Defence,* edited by Henry Cotton, Vols. 1 and 2. Oxford: University Press, 1862.

Walsh, Mary E. *The Wine of Roman Babylon.* Nashville: Southern Publishing Association, 1945. 223 pages.

Warren, F. E. *The Liturgy and Ritual of the Ante-Nicene Church,* 2d ed., revised. London: Society for Promoting Christian Knowledge, 1912. 317 pages.

Wesley, John. *Explanatory Notes Upon the New Testament.* London: John Mason, 1831. Vol. 2.

——. *The Journal of the Rev. John Wesley.* Everyman's Edition; London: J. M. Dent and Sons, 1913.

White, James. *Life Sketches. Ancestry, Early Life, Christian Experience, and Extensive Labors, of Elder James White, and His Wife, Mrs. Ellen G. White.* Battle Creek, Michigan: Steam Press of the Seventh-day Adventist Publishing Association, 1880. 416 pages.

Williams, Egerton R. *Hill Towns of Italy.* New York: Houghton Mifflin, 1903.

Wilson, L. C. *The History of Sprinkling.* Cincinnati, Ohio: Standard Publishing Company, 1895. 152 pages.

# Index of Text

# Index of Illustrations